REVISING & ED

3RD GRADE

By: Carlin Liborio

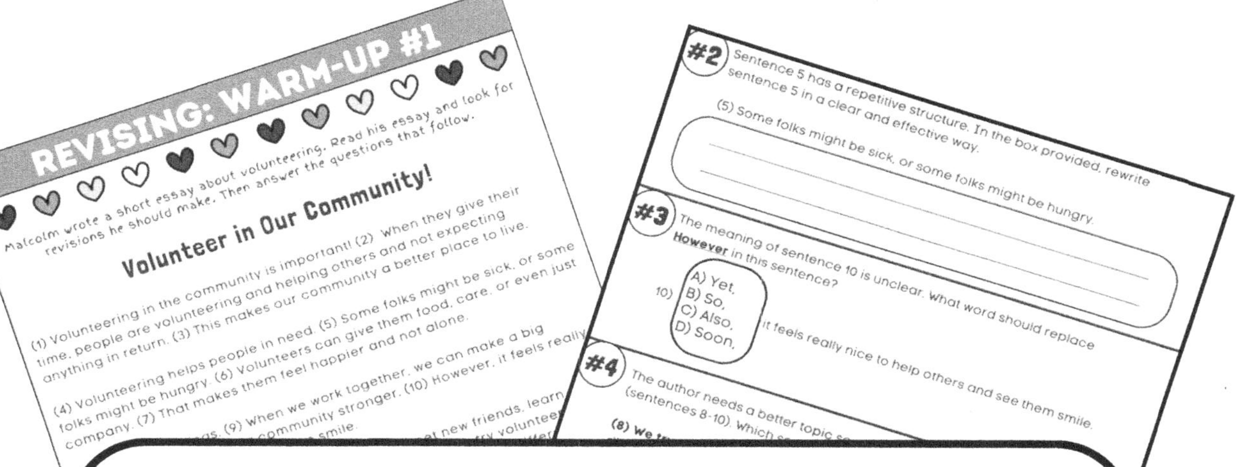

7 weeks of Revising &

7 weeks of Editing

Warm-Ups

5 Questions Each!

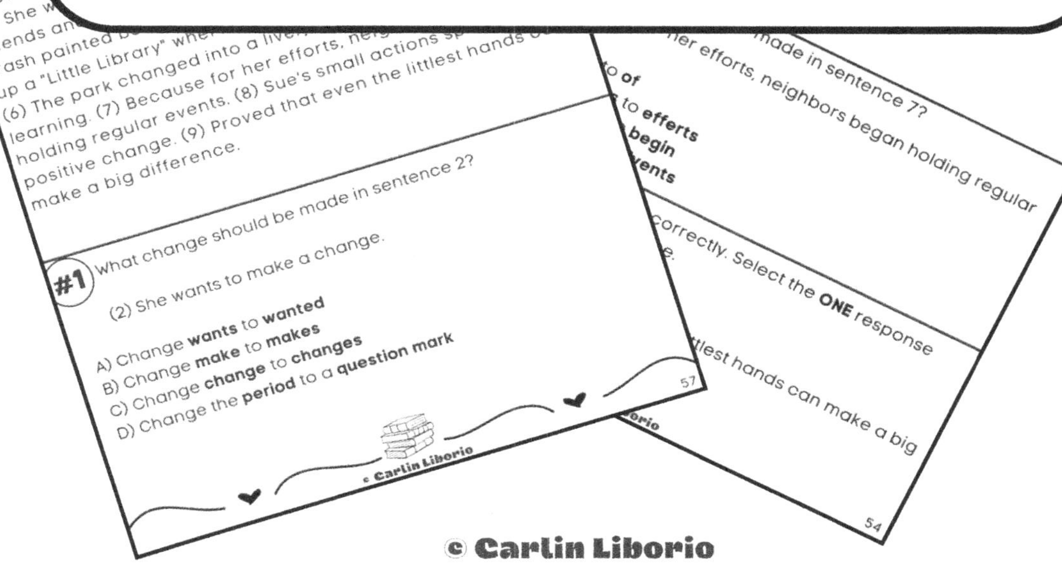

Cross-Curricular
Social Studies & Science Passages!

REVISING: PRACTICE #1

Mai wrote about the day she and her best friend, Jenny, volunteered at the local animal shelter. Read Mai's story and look for revisions she needs to make. Then answer the questions that follow.

Saturday at the Animal Shelter

(1) Jenny and I love animals very much, and one Saturday, we decided to spend our day volunteering at the Happy Paws Animal Shelter. (2) When we arrived, the kind people at the shelter welcomed us with big smiles. (3) They gave us aprons and showed us around. (4) There were dogs, cats, bunnies, and even some little hamsters. (5) Each animal had a story.

(6) We went to an area. (7) There were dogs of all sizes and colors. (8) Jenny and I helped clean their cages, and then we took some dogs for a walk. (9) We loved how happy the dogs looked when they got to stretch them and play.

(10) After playing with the dogs, Jenny and I went to the cat room. (11) There were so many cute kittens and grown-up cats. (12) We cleaned their litter boxes and gave them different water and food.

(13) We moved on. (14) There were fluffy bunnies with floppy ears, and they were adorable. (15) Jenny and I cleaned their cages and gave them fresh hay to eat. (16) Giggled we did as hopped and nibbled on the hay the bunnies.

(17) Finally, we went to the hamster corner. (18) There were tiny hamsters with tiny paws. (19) Jenny and I helped clean their cages and gave them some fresh bedding.

(20) At lunchtime, we talked about how much fun we were having and how happy we were to help the animals. (21) We talked about our favorite animals. (22) Jenny ate only half of her sandwich. (23) We even made plans to come back and volunteer again soon.

(24) After lunch, we continued to help at the shelter. (25) We washed dishes, swept the floors, and made sure everythi... at the shelter were so gratef...

(27) As the day came to a... helped that day. (28) We l... made a difference in the...

(29) Jenny and I knew tha... animals at the Happy Paw... just kids, we can make a b... just kids.

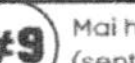

#8 Which sentence would **BEST** follow and support sentence 19?

(17) Finally, we went to the hamster corner. (18) There were tiny hamsters with tiny paws. (19) Jenny and I helped clean their cages and gave them some fresh bedding.

A) Hamsters are similar to gerbils.
B) The hamsters ran on their little wheels, making us laugh.
C) Being prey for so many animals, it's no wonder that most hamsters are nocturnal.
D) By gnawing, hamsters keep their teeth nice and sharp.

#9 Mai has included a sentence that does not belong in the sixth paragraph (sentences 20-23). Which sentence should she remove?

(20) At lunchtime, we talked about how much fun we were having and how happy we were to help the animals. (21) We talked about which animals were our favorites. (22) Jenny ate only half of her sandwich. (23) We even made plans to come back and volunteer again soon.

A) Sentence 20
B) Sentence 21
C) Sentence 22
D) Sentence 23

#10 Sentence 30 repeats information. In the box provided, rewrite sentence 29 in a clear and effective way.

...just kids, we can make a big ...ugh we are just kids.

16

7 weeks of Revising &
7 weeks of Editing
Practice Pages
10 Questions Each!

EDI...

Max is writing a st... Read this parag... corrections he need...

(1) Sue noticed her neighborhood park was littered and dull. (2) She wants to make a change. (3) She gathered her friends and organized a cleanup day. (4) They collected trash painted benches, and planted flowers. (5) Sue also set up a "Little Library" where kid's could exchange books. (6) The park changed into a lively place of laughter and learning. (7) Because for her efforts, neighbors began holding regular events. (8) Sue's small actions sparked a positive change. (9) Proved that even the littlest hands can make a big difference.

#1 What change should be made in sentence 2?

(2) She wants to make a change.

A) Change **wants** to **wanted**
B) Change **make** to **makes**
C) Change **change** to **changes**
D) Change the period to a question mark

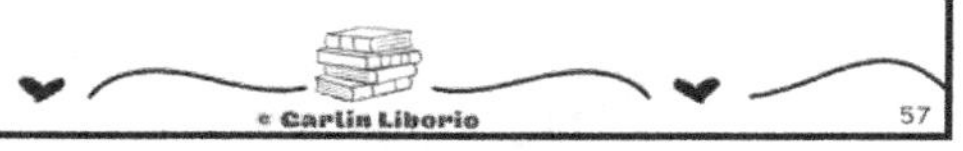

© Carlin Liborio 57

...ce 4?

...s, and planted

#3 What change should be made in sentence 5?

(5) Sue also set up a "Little Library" where kid's could exchange books.

A) Change **up** to **in**
B) Change **where** to **when**
C) Change **kid's** to **kids**
D) Change **could** to **couldn't**

#4 What change should be made in sentence 7?

(7) Because for her efforts, neighbors began holding regular events.

A) Change **for** to **of**
B) Change **efforts** to **efferts**
C) Change **began** to **begin**
D) Change **events** to **Events**

#5 Sentence 9 is written incorrectly. Select the **ONE** response that corrects this sentence.

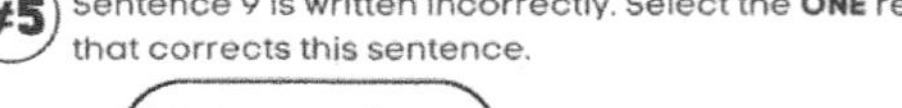

(9) [A) And proved. That / B) This proved that / C) Learning about that / D) This proved it. That] even the littlest hands can make a big difference.

© Carlin Liborio 58

Revising & Editing Student Workbook – 3rd Grade:
English Language Arts – 14 Weeks of Daily Warm-Ups + Practice

ISBN 979-8-9985258-6-5

Join my email list for FREEBIES and tips!

Reading & Writing FREEBIES, important information, and more!

https://carlinliborio.myflodesk.com

Looking for more resources and support?

Follow my teacher Facebook page, subscribe to my YouTube Channel, and sign up for online courses!

https://CarlinLiborio.com

Interested in a purchase order?

Email me for a quote for your campus or district! Discounts on class sets!

Carlin@CarlinLiborio.com

About this Workbook

- This student workbook contains **daily revising and editing warm-up and practice pages** for **third-grade** students.

- The passages are **cross-curricular** and integrated with **social studies and science TEKS** (Texas Essential Knowledge and Skills) for **3rd grade**.

- The **passages** include **warm-up and practice pages** along with **answer keys**. You may want to remove the answer keys before giving this workbook to students.

- Students can **write directly on the pages** and keep all their warm-ups and practice pages **neatly organized** in **one book**.

- Each student can **practice revising and editing skills directly in their own book**.

- Students can also use their workbook to look back at **previous questions as a review of what they have learned throughout the year.**

Workbook Contents:

Part 1: REVISING

7 Weeks of Warm-Up & Practice <u>STUDENT PAGES</u>

Each week contains:

- A revising **Warm-Up Passage with five questions**
- A revising **Practice Passage with ten questions**

Part 2: EDITING

7 Weeks of Warm-Up & Practice <u>STUDENT PAGES</u>

Each week contains:

- An Editing **Warm-Up Passage with five questions**
- Two Editing **Practice Passages with five questions each (ten questions total)**

Arms/Cups Strategy Cards

Answer Keys for Revising & Editing Warm-Ups and Practice Questions can be found at the back of the book.

**Note: You may remove the answer keys at the back of the book or keep them for students to self-check.

About this Workbook

Why should you use cross-curricular passages integrated with social studies and science?

- This gives students **background knowledge** to help them with **reading comprehension**.
- By integrating **social studies and/or science** with reading and writing, students will **develop high-level academic vocabulary**.
- Students will **make connections across subjects** and recognize the **importance of writing in all subject areas.**
- **Connecting ideas across disciplines** helps students construct knowledge more actively, leading to a **better understanding and retention** of the material.
- Students also benefit from these **time-saving learning opportunities** by seeing how **different subjects are connected**, which provides a **new perspective on learning.**

Instructions for Use:

WARM-UP (STUDENT PAGES):

- Use this as a weekly warm-up and do one revising question each day (Monday - Friday).
- In the beginning, model questions for the students. Next, they can answer them in pairs or groups, share answers, and discuss/check.
- You could do **seven weeks of revising warm-ups** followed by **seven weeks of editing warm-ups**, or you could alternate **one week of revising warm- ups** and **one week of editing warm-ups**.
- There are **14 weeks** of daily revising and editing warm-up questions.
- Have each student write in their own workbook.
- You could also use the warm-up as a **shortened assignment.**

PRACTICE (STUDENT PAGES):

- **Teacher Table/Small Group/Tutoring** - Have students do the workbook practice pages at your teacher table while you coach and guide. Give more support to students who need it and more independence to advanced students, providing them with regular feedback.
- **Whole Group** - Another option is to complete the questions as a class. Have students justify their answers in groups and explain why their choices improve the writing. Then, remind them to apply those choices to their own compositions.
- **Station/Assignment/Practice** - Assign students the workbook practice pages as a station independently or with a buddy/group. You can check their answers or provide an answer key for self-checking.

Part 1: Revising

Revising Strategies:

- Highlight the key words in the question.
- Highlight the sentence or paragraph in the passage.
- Read the sentence/paragraph out loud (or use a whisper phone).
- Try each answer choice.
- Eliminate/cross out answers that do not make sense.
- Choose the answer that makes the most sense.
- Lastly, justify your answer!

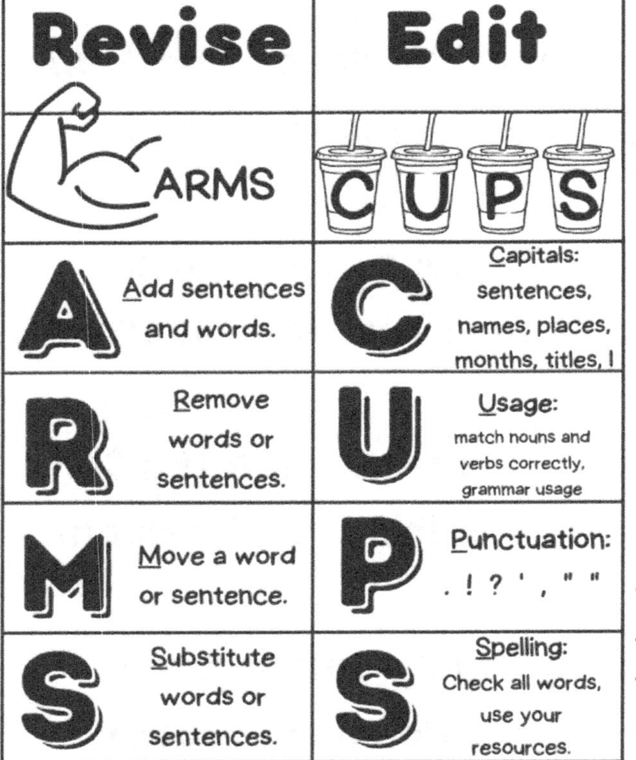

What is REVISING?

- Revising is the **effectiveness** of your writing. Is it **effective**?
- Revising is adding, removing, moving, or substituting words or sentences to make your writing **BETTER**!
- Revising is **reviewing** and **improving** your writing!

REVISING: WARM-UP #1

Malcolm wrote a short essay about volunteering. Read his essay and look for revisions he should make. Then answer the questions that follow.

Volunteer in Our Community!

(1) Volunteering in the community is important! (2) When they give their time, people are volunteering and helping others and not expecting anything in return. (3) This makes our community a better place to live.

(4) Volunteering helps people in need. (5) Some folks might be sick, or some folks might be hungry. (6) Volunteers can give them food, care, or even just company. (7) That makes them feel happier and not alone.

(8) We try new things. (9) When we work together, we can make a big difference and make our community stronger. (10) However, it feels really nice to help others and see them smile.

(11) Lastly, volunteering can be fun! You can meet new friends, learn new things, and have great adventures. (12) So, if you can, try volunteering in your community. (13) It's a small thing that can make a big difference.

 What is the **BEST** way to revise sentence 2?

(2) When they give their time, people are volunteering and helping others and not expecting anything in return.

A) Without expecting to volunteer or anything in return, when they give their time and help others.
B) When people volunteer, they give their time and help others without expecting anything in return.
C) People give their time when they volunteer without expecting anything in return when they help others.
D) When people volunteer without expecting anything in return, they give their time and help others.

#2 Sentence 5 has a repetitive structure. In the box provided, rewrite sentence 5 in a clear and effective way.

(5) Some folks might be sick, or some folks might be hungry.

____

____

#3 The meaning of sentence 10 is unclear. What word should replace **<u>However</u>** in this sentence?

10) [A) Yet, / B) So, / C) Also, / D) Soon,] it feels really nice to help others and see them smile.

A) Yet,
B) So,
C) Also,
D) Soon,

#4 The author needs a better topic sentence for the third paragraph (sentences 8-10). Which sentence should replace sentence 8?

(8) We try new things. (9) When we work together, we can make a big difference and make our community stronger. (10) However, it feels really nice to help others and see them smile.

A) Volunteering in the community means a lot.
B) Making a big difference in the community is what volunteering is all about.
C) Volunteering is a great way to make friends.
D) Volunteering teaches us values like kindness and teamwork.

#5 Which sentence would **BEST** follow and support sentence 13?

(11) Lastly, volunteering can be fun! You can meet new friends, learn new things, and have great adventures. (12) So, if you can, try volunteering in your community. (13) It's a small thing that can make a big difference.

A) You'll feel proud of yourself for helping out.
B) That's all I have to say about volunteering.
C) Volunteering can be really fun!
D) If you don't have time to volunteer, maybe you can donate money instead.

REVISING: PRACTICE #1

Mai wrote about the day she and her best friend, Jenny, volunteered at the local animal shelter. Read Mai's story and look for revisions she needs to make. Then answer the questions that follow.

Saturday at the Animal Shelter

(1) Jenny and I love animals very much, and one Saturday, we decided to spend our day volunteering at the Happy Paws Animal Shelter. (2) When we arrived, the kind people at the shelter welcomed us with big smiles. (3) They gave us aprons and showed us around. (4) There were dogs, cats, bunnies, and even some little hamsters. (5) Each animal had a story.

(6) We went to an area. (7) There were dogs of all sizes and colors. (8) Jenny and I helped clean their cages, and then we took some dogs for a walk. (9) We loved how happy the dogs looked when they got to stretch them and play.

(10) After playing with the dogs, Jenny and I went to the cat room. (11) There were so many cute kittens and grown-up cats. (12) We cleaned their litter boxes and gave them different water and food.

(13) We moved on. (14) There were fluffy bunnies with floppy ears, and they were adorable. (15) Jenny and I cleaned their cages and gave them fresh hay to eat. (16) Giggled we did as hopped and nibbled on the hay the bunnies.

(17) Finally, we went to the hamster corner. (18) There were tiny hamsters with tiny paws. (19) Jenny and I helped clean their cages and gave them some fresh bedding.

(20) At lunchtime, we talked about how much fun we were having and how happy we were to help the animals. (21) We talked about our favorite animals. (22) Jenny ate only half of her sandwich. (23) We even made plans to come back and volunteer again soon.

(24) After lunch, we continued to help at the shelter. (25) We washed dishes, swept the floors, and made sure everything was clean and cozy for the animals. (26) The people at the shelter were so grateful for our help.

(27) As the day came to an end, Jenny and I said goodbye to all the animals we had helped that day. (28) We left the shelter with our hearts full of joy, knowing we had made a difference in the lives of the furry friends we had met.

(29) Jenny and I knew that we would always have a special place in our hearts for the animals at the Happy Paws Animal Shelter. (30) We learned that even though we are just kids, we can make a big difference by helping those in need, even though we are just kids.

PRACTICE #1 QUESTIONS

Which sentence would **BEST** follow and support sentence 5?

(1) Jenny and I love animals very much, and one Saturday, we decided to spend our day volunteering at the Happy Paws Animal Shelter. (2) When we arrived, the kind people at the shelter welcomed us with big smiles. (3) They gave us aprons and showed us around. (4) There were dogs, cats, bunnies, and even some little hamsters. (5) Each animal had a story.

A) Jenny's mom drove us to the shelter.
B) Jenny and I wanted to help them all.
C) I wondered what time lunch would be.
D) Jenny had visited the animal shelter once before.

Mai needs a better topic sentence for the second paragraph (sentences 6-9). Which sentence should replace sentence 6?

(6) We went to an area. (7) There were dogs of all sizes and colors.

A) First, we arrived at the animal shelter.
B) There were all kinds of animals.
C) The shelter workers were so friendly.
D) First, we went to the dog area.

The meaning of sentence 9 is unclear. What phrase should replace **them** in this sentence?

(9) We loved how happy the dogs looked when they got to stretch them and play.

A) the dogs'
B) Jenny and Mai
C) the animals
D) their legs

The meaning of sentence 12 is unclear. What word should replace **different** in this sentence?

(12) We cleaned their litter boxes and gave them water and food.

A) fresh
B) flavored
C) wet
D) hot

Which sentence would **BEST** follow and support sentence 12?

(10) After playing with the dogs, Jenny and I went to the cat room. (11) There were so many cute kittens and grown-up cats. (12) We cleaned their litter boxes and gave them different water and food.

A) I'm really more of a dog person, though.
B) The cats purred and rubbed their soft fur against our legs, thanking us.
C) Jenny said, "There are so many kittens and adult cats!"
D) That day, we saw many animals, including dogs, cats, bunnies and hamsters.

Mai needs a better topic sentence for the fourth paragraph (sentences 13-16). Which sentence should replace sentence 13?

(13) We moved on. (14) There were fluffy bunnies with floppy ears, and they were adorable. (15) Jenny and I cleaned their cages and gave them fresh hay to eat. (16) Giggled we did as hopped and nibbled on the hay the bunnies.

A) Next, we visited the bunnies.
B) That's what we did with the cats.
C) I have more to tell you.
D) What a fun day it was for us!

What is the **BEST** way to revise sentence 16?

(16) Giggled we did as hopped and nibbled on the hay the bunnies.

A) The bunnies giggled as we hopped around and nibbled on the hay.
B) We giggled as the hay hopped around and nibbled on the bunnies.
C) The hay giggled as we hopped around and nibbled on the bunnies.
D) We giggled as the bunnies hopped around and nibbled on the hay.

Which sentence would **BEST** follow and support sentence 19?

(17) Finally, we went to the hamster corner. (18) There were tiny hamsters with tiny paws. (19) Jenny and I helped clean their cages and gave them some fresh bedding.

A) Hamsters are similar to gerbils.
B) The hamsters ran on their little wheels, making us laugh.
C) Being prey for so many animals, it's no wonder that most hamsters are nocturnal.
D) By gnawing, hamsters keep their teeth nice and sharp.

Mai has included a sentence that does not belong in the sixth paragraph (sentences 20-23). Which sentence should she remove?

(20) At lunchtime, we talked about how much fun we were having and how happy we were to help the animals. (21) We talked about which animals were our favorites. (22) Jenny ate only half of her sandwich. (23) We even made plans to come back and volunteer again soon.

A) Sentence 20
B) Sentence 21
C) Sentence 22
D) Sentence 23

Sentence 30 repeats information. In the box provided, rewrite sentence 29 in a clear and effective way.

(30) We learned that even though we are just kids, we can make a big difference by helping those in need, even though we are just kids.

____

____

____

REVISING: WARM-UP #2

Paul wrote a short essay about making a budget. Read the essay and look for revisions he should make. Then answer the questions that follow.

Creating a Simple Budget

(1) Creating a simple budget is making a plan for your money. (2) You can have some money for spending. (3) Some for saving and some for donating. (4) Here's how you can make your own budget:

(5) First, think about how much money you have. (6) This can be your allowance, money you get, or gifts. (7) Write down that amount as your "Total Income."

(8) Next, decide how much money you want to spend. (9) This includes things like toys, snacks, or games. (10) People spend a lot on these things around the holidays. (11) Write down this amount as your "Spending Money."

(12) Do this now. It's important to save some money for later. (13) Saving is like keeping some coins in your piggy bank. (14) You can save for something special or for emergencies. (15) Write down how much you want to save as your "Saving Goal."

(16) Lastly, think about helping others. (17) Donating means giving some of your money to people or causes that need it. (18) You can choose a charity or a friend who needs help.

(19) Now, your budget is ready! (20) Remember to keep track of your spending, saving, and donating. (21) It's a great way to learn about money and make a difference.

#1 Combine sentences 2 and 3 in a clear and effective way.

(2) You can have some money for spending. (3) Some for saving and some for donating.

____

____

$

The meaning of sentence 6 is unclear. What word should replace **get** in this sentence?

(6) This can be your allowance, money you
A) take,
B) give,
C) borrow,
D) earn,
or gifts.

Paul has included a sentence that does not belong in the third paragraph (sentences 8-11). Which sentence should he remove?

(8) Next, decide how much money you want to spend. (9) This includes things like toys, snacks, or games. (10) People spend a lot on these things around the holidays. (11) Write down this amount as your "Spending Money."

A) Sentence 8
B) Sentence 9
C) Sentence 10
D) Sentence 11

Paul needs a better topic sentence for the fourth paragraph (sentences 12-15). Which sentence should replace sentence 12?

(12) Do this now. It's important to save some money for later. (13) Saving is like keeping some coins in your piggy bank. (14) You can save for something special or for emergencies. (15) Write down how much you want to save as your "Saving Goal."

A) It's important to save some money for later.
B) Anyone can make a budget.
C) There can be three parts of a budget: saving, spending, and donating.
D) Without a budget, you may find yourself wondering where your money went.

Which sentence would **BEST** follow and support sentence 18?

(16) Lastly, think about helping others. (17) Donating means giving some of your money to people or causes that need it. (18) You can choose a charity or a friend who needs help.

A) Your budget is now ready to go!
B) Write down the amount you want to donate as your "Donation Fund."
C) Budgeting is a valuable skill to learn while you are young.
D) Explore how much you can set aside each month for a long-term savings goal.

REVISING: PRACTICE #2

Danna wrote a story about making her first budget. Read Danna's story and look for revisions she should make. Then answer the questions that follow.

My First Budget

(1) I wanted to learn about money, so I decided to make a budget. (2) It was important. (3) The first thing I did was talk to my parents about it. (4) They were happy that I wanted to do money, and they said they would help me.

(5) We sat down at the kitchen table, and my mom explained the budgeting basics. (6) She said a budget should have three parts: spending, saving, and donating. (7) Spending is for things I want or need right now, like toys or snacks. (8) Saving is for the future, such as when I want to buy a nice bike. (9) Donating helps others, like giving money to a charity to help others.

(10) For the spending part of my budget, I thought about the things I really wanted. (11) I like getting new books, so I decided to use some money for that. (12) I also like going to the movies with my friends, so I included that too. (13) My mom helped me to know how much I should spend on each of these things so I wouldn't run out of money too quickly.

(14) We worked on something. (15) It was important. (16) I knew I wanted a new bike, so we talked about how much it would cost. (17) My mom helped me break it down into smaller amounts I could save each month. (18) It felt good to know I was working toward a big goal, and I even made a chart to track my progress.

(19) Really special to me was the part of my budget for donating. (20) I wanted to help animals, so my mom suggested we find a local animal shelter to support. (21) We decided to set aside some money each month to buy food and toys for the shelter animals. (22) I felt so happy knowing I could make something for their lives.

(23) As I started using my budget, I learned some important things. (24) I learned to make choices about how I spend my money. (25) I don't need to buy everything I want right away. (26) Saving for my bike is exciting, and I knew it will be worth it in the end. (27) Donating to the animal shelter makes me feel helpful. (28) I will assist others in need.

(29) Creating a budget turned out to be a fun and valuable thing to do. (30) It made me feel responsible and smart about my money. (31) Plus, I learned that even as a kid, by giving back, I can make a positive impact on the world by giving back. (32) So, if you ever want to be good with money, just remember to make a budget with spending, saving, and donating parts. (33) It's a great way to learn! (34) It's a great way to make a difference!

PRACTICE #2 QUESTIONS

Which sentence should replace sentence 2 to **BEST** state the central idea of this paper?

(1) I wanted to learn about money, so I decided to make a budget. **(2) It was important.** (3) The first thing I did was talk to my parents about it. (4) They were happy that I wanted to do money, and they said they would help me.

A) I knew that budgeting could allow me to use my extra money toward something I needed or wanted.
B) I didn't really know exactly where to begin.
C) A budget is a plan for your money, and I wanted to be really good at using my money wisely.
D) My parents seemed to be pretty good with money, and I hoped they would help me.

The meaning of sentence 4 is unclear. What phrase should replace <u>**do**</u> in this sentence?

(4) They were happy that I wanted to [A) learn about / B) save up / C) spend some / D) share my] money, and they said they would help me.

A) learn about
B) save up
C) spend some
D) share my

Sentence 9 repeats information. In the box provided, rewrite sentence 9 in a clear and effective way.

(9) Donating helps others, like giving money to a charity to help others.

____

____

____

The meaning of sentence 13 is unclear. What phrase should replace **know** in this sentence?

(13) My mom helped me to
A) ask around
B) figure out
C) be curious
D) pay no attention to
how much I should spend on each of these things so I won't run out of money too quickly.

Danna needs a better topic sentence for the fourth paragraph (sentences 14-18). Which sentence should replace sentences 14 and 15?

(14) We worked on something. (15) It was important.

A) When buying a bike, it's important to choose the right size.
B) Next, we worked on the saving part of my budget.
C) My mom helped me with this next part.
D) Making a budget is not that hard once you get used to it.

What is the **BEST** way to revise sentence 19?

(19) Really special to me was the part of my budget for donating.

A) The donating part of my budget was really special to me.
B) The really special part of my donating was the budget part.
C) The really special donating part to me was the budget.
D) Really special to me was for the donating part of my budget.

The meaning of sentence 22 is unclear. What phrase should replace **something for** in this sentence?

(22) I felt so happy knowing I could make
A) a few dollars for
B) a lot of confusion in
C) more things to do with
D) a difference in
their lives.

What is the **BEST** way to combine sentences 27 and 28?

(27) Donating to the animal shelter makes me feel helpful. (28) I will assist others in need.

A) Donating to the animal shelter makes me feel helpful, so I will assist others in need.
B) Donating to the animal shelter makes me feel helpful because I will assist others in need.
C) Even though donating to the animal shelter makes me feel helpful, I am assisting others in need.
D) Donating to the animal shelter makes me feel helpful, yet I am assisting others in need.

Sentence 31 repeats information. In the box provided, rewrite sentence 31 in a clear and effective way.

(31) Plus, I learned that even as a kid, by giving back, I can make a positive impact on the world by giving back.

____

____

____

What is the **BEST** way to combine sentences 33 and 34?

(33) It's a great way to learn! (34) It's a great way to make a difference!

A) It's a great way to learn and make a difference!
B) It's a great way to learn, but it's also a great way to make a difference!
C) It's a great way to learn, and it's a great way to make a difference!
D) Since it's a great way to learn, it's a great way to make a difference!

REVISING: WARM-UP #3

Kerry wrote a short essay about some of Benjamin Franklin's contributions. Read the essay and see what revisions she should make. Then answer the questions that follow.

Benjamin Franklin's Community

(1) Benjamin Franklin was an important leader in the 1700s. (2) He guided his local community in many ways. (3) He also guided his nation in many ways. (4) With amazing intelligence and leadership skills, he played a major role in the country's early history.

(5) During the American Revolution, Franklin showed great leadership during the American Revolution. (6) He had a special job dealing with other nations and getting their support. (7) He worked well with leaders in Europe, especially France. (8) He played a key role in the success of the American fight for independence.

(9) Franklin worked hard to create the U.S. Constitution. (10) His stuff helped form our American democracy. (11) The Constitution, which he helped create, remains the central part of our government. (12) To this day, it guides our nation.

(13) Improve the local community Franklin did a lot to. (14) He helped start the first volunteer fire department. (15) He worked to improve street lighting and public health programs, making his neighborhood safer and more livable. (16) His efforts helped create the Philadelphia Library to provide knowledge to his community.

(17) Benjamin Franklin did a lot for his nation and community. (18) His wisdom was important. (19) His leadership was also important.

#1 Kerry wants to combine the ideas in sentences 2 and 3. In the space provided write the sentences in a clear and effective way.

(2) He guided his local community in many ways. 3) He also guided his nation in many ways.

____

____

#2 Sentence 5 repeats information and needs to be revised. In the space provided, rewrite sentence 5 in a clear and effective way.

(5) During the American Revolution, Franklin showed great leadership during the American Revolution.

____

____

#3 The word stuff is not the right word for sentence 10. Which phrase should replace **stuff** in this sentence?

(10) His [A) wise advice / B) bad ideas / C) old-fashioned clothes / D) wife's belongings] helped form our American democracy.

A) wise advice
B) bad ideas
C) old-fashioned clothes
D) wife's belongings

#4 What is the **BEST** way to revise sentence 13?

(13) Improve the local community Franklin did a lot to.

A) Improve the local community did a lot to Franklin.
B) The local community did a lot to improve Franklin.
C) Improve the local community a lot Franklin did.
D) Franklin did a lot to improve the local community.

#5 What is the **BEST** way to combine the ideas in sentences 18 and 19?

(18) His wisdom was important. (19) His leadership was also important.

A) His wisdom was important, so his leadership was also important.
B) His wisdom and leadership were important.
C) His wisdom was important, and his leadership was also important.
D) They were important, his wisdom and leadership.

REVISING: PRACTICE #3

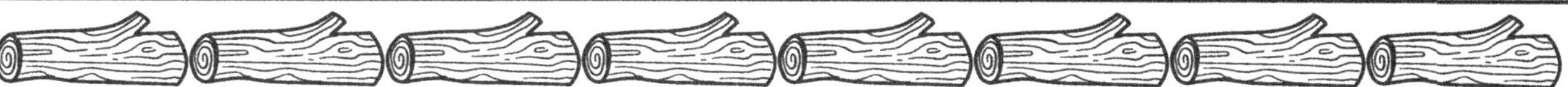

Lakisha wrote an essay about the community and contributions of Daniel Boone. Read her essay and see what revisions she should make. Then answer the questions that follow.

Daniel Boone and His New Community

(1) Daniel Boone was brave and loved adventures. (2) He lived in the 1700s in America. (3) He did something amazing and important.

(4) Long ago, there was a big forest in America, and people didn't live there because it was too wild. (5) There were no houses or towns. (6) But different Daniel Boone was. (7) He loved going and wanted to discover a new place to live.

(8) Daniel packed up his things and walked into the forest. (9) He traveled very far, crossed rivers, and climbed mountains. (10) It was not easy, but he was determined. (11) Along the way, he met Native Americans. (12) They taught him how to survive in the wild.

(13) Daniel found a beautiful valley. (14) It was between two big mountains. (15) It had rich soil, clear streams, and lots of animals. (16) Daniel knew this was the good place for his new community.

(17) He started by clearing the land and building log cabins. (18) More people heard about this special place. (19) They decided to join Daniel's community. (20) Worked together they all did to make it a safe and happy place to live.

(21) To protect themselves, they built a fort to protect themselves. (22) The fort was named after Daniel Boone. (23) It kept them safe from wild animals and unfriendly neighbors. (24) Daniel was the leader of the community. (25) He helped solve problems and make important decisions.

(26) One day, some Native Americans came to talk to Daniel. (27) They were worried about the settlers taking their land. (28) Daniel Boone respected the Native Americans. (29) He talked to them and made a thing. (30) They decided to share the land and live together in peace.

(31) Life in the fort was hard, but it got better. (32) More families came to live there, and the town grew. (33) Today, a state park and museum are located on the old fort site. (34) They built schools for kids to learn and churches for worship.

(35) Daniel Boone's dream of creating a new community had come true. (36) He turned a wild forest into a safe and happy place. (37) Boone’s fort became a symbol of bravery, teamwork, and the American spirit.

(38) Daniel Boone created a new community in the wild, untamed land of America. (39) He showed us that with determination and working together, we can make amazing things happen!

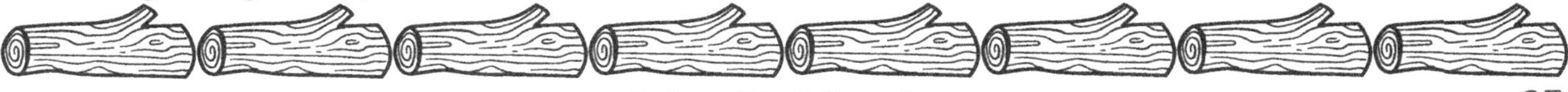

PRACTICE #3 QUESTIONS

Which sentence should replace sentence 3 to **BEST** state the central idea of this paper?

(1) Daniel Boone was brave and loved adventures. (2) He lived in the 1700s in America. **(3) He did something amazing and important.**

A) He was born on Oct. 22, 1734 and had 10 brothers and sisters.
B) He created a brand new community in the wild, untamed land.
C) Many stories have been told and books have been written about him.
D) He fought in one of the last battles of the Revolutionary War.

Sentence 6 needs to be revised. In the space provided, rewrite sentence 6 in a clear and effective way.

(6) But different Daniel Boone was.

____

____

____

#3 The meaning of sentence 7 is unclear. What word should replace **going** in this sentence?

(7) He loved [A) leaving / B) escaping / C) exploring / D) staying] and wanted to discover a new place to live.

A) leaving
B) escaping
C) exploring
D) staying

Which sentence would **BEST** follow and support sentence 12?

(8) Daniel packed up his things and walked into the forest. (9) He traveled very far, crossed rivers, and climbed mountains. (10) It was not easy, but he was determined. (11) Along the way, he met Native Americans. (12) They taught him how to survive in the wild.

A) They showed him how to find food, build shelters, and take care of the land.
B) At this time, Boone wasn't famous and was unknown to most people.
C) A few years later, Boone fought in the American Revolutionary War.
D) Some Native Americans considered Boone and other hunters to be intruders.

What is the **BEST** way to combine sentences 13 and 14?

(13) Daniel found a beautiful valley. (14) It was between two big mountains.

A) Daniel found a beautiful valley, and the valley was between two big mountains.
B) Daniel found a beautiful valley between two big mountains.
C) Between two big mountains it was that Daniel found a beautiful valley.
D) A beautiful valley Daniel found, and two big mountains it was between.

The meaning of sentence 16 is unclear. What word should replace **good** in this sentence?

(16) Daniel knew this was the [A) nearest / B) farthest / C) perfect / D) flattest] place for his new community.

What is the **BEST** way to revise sentence 20?

(20) Worked together they all did to make it a safe and happy place to live.

A) To make it a safe and also a happy place to live, they all worked together.
B) A safe and happy place to live all worked together they all did.
C) Worked all together they to make it a safe and happy place to live.
D) They all worked together to make it a safe and happy place to live.

Sentence 21 repeats information. In the box provided, rewrite sentence 21 in a clear and effective way.

(21) To protect themselves, they built a fort to protect themselves.

____

____

____

The meaning of sentence 29 is unclear. What phrase should replace **thing** in this sentence?

(29) He talked to them and made a

A) peaceful agreement.
B) nice lunch.
C) happy parade.
D) violent conflict.

#10 Lakisha has included a sentence that does not belong in the eighth paragraph (sentences 31-34). Which sentence should she remove?

(31) Life in the fort was hard, but it got better. (32) More families came to live there, and the town grew. (33) Today, a state park and museum are located on the old fort site. (34) They built schools for kids to learn and churches for worship.

A) Sentence 31
B) Sentence 32
C) Sentence 33
D) Sentence 34

REVISING: WARM-UP #4

Diego wrote a short essay about a cultural celebration he knows. Read the essay and see what revisions he should make. Then answer the questions that follow.

Day of the Dead (Día de los Muertos)

(1) The Day of the Dead is a celebration that takes place in Mexico and other communities around the world. (2) This is a big deal.

(3) During this time, families create beautiful altars with colorful flowers, shiny candles, and delicious food during this time. (4) They also make colorful paper decorations called papel picado. (5) Families go to the graves of their loved ones to clean them and put pretty flowers there. (6) When they visit the graves, they tell stories and remember all the good times they had with the people who passed away.

(7) People also like to dress up in fun costumes with colorful skeleton faces. (8) It's not meant to be scary. (9) It's like a lively party. (10) It's like a joyful party. (11) These costumes show that even though we all eventually pass away, we still celebrate life and remember them.

(12) The Day of the Dead is a special time for families to be close, a special time to eat yummy food, and a special time to share stories. (13) It helps everyone remember where they come from and the love that will always be in their hearts for the people who are no longer here. (14) This holiday brings happiness and colorful traditions to remember our loved ones.

Which sentence should replace sentence 2 to **BEST** state the central idea of this paper?

(1) The Day of the Dead is a celebration that takes place in Mexico and in other communities around the world. **(2) This is a big deal.**

A) Day of the Dead is a celebration, and it takes place at the beginning of November.
B) This holiday is important because it helps people remember their family and friends who have passed.
C) This holiday comes from Mexico, is very popular, and is celebrated in Mexico and other parts of the world.
D) Day of the Dead is interesting, and I'm going to tell you all about it now, so be sure to keep reading.

#2 Sentence 3 repeats information. In the box provided, rewrite sentence 3 in a clear and effective way.

(3) During this time, families create beautiful altars with colorful flowers, shiny candles, and delicious food during this time.

____

____

#3 What is the **BEST** way to combine sentences 9 and 10?

(9) It's like a lively party. (10) It's like a joyful party.

A) It's like a party that's lively and also a joyful party.
B) It's like a lively, joyful party.
C) A lively, joyful party it's like.
D) It's like a party, and it's lively, and it's joyful.

#4 The meaning of sentence 11 is unclear. What phrase should replace <u>**them**</u> in this sentence?

(11) These costumes show that even though we all eventually pass away, we still celebrate life and remember

A) skeleton faces.
B) colorful costumes.
C) those we love.
D) happy parties.

#5 Sentence 12 repeats information. In the box provided, rewrite sentence 12 in a clear and effective way.

12) The Day of the Dead is a special time for families to be close, a special time to eat yummy food, and a special time to share stories.

____

____

REVISING: PRACTICE #4

Kyle wrote a story about his cousin and a festival he loves. Read the story and see what revisions he should make. Then answer the questions that follow.

A Unique Vietnamese Festival

(1) Linh's eyes lit up as she heard that Le Vu Lan, the Vietnamese festival, had come once again. (2) She knew that this celebration was a time to remember and honor her ancestors, especially her grandparents who had lived in Vietnam. (3) Although she was born in America, Linh's family keeps their Vietnamese traditions.

(4) Like a big family reunion the festival was for Linh. (5) The entire family came together at the temple, and it was quite a sight! (6) The temple was beautifully decorated with things. (7) Linh was filled with joy when she saw the lanterns. (8) They came in all shapes and sizes. (9) The lanterns are believed to guide the spirits of ancestors back to visit their loved ones.

(10) They did things to prepare. (11) There were spring rolls, steaming bowls of noodles, and many fresh fruits. (12) They believed that by offering these foods, their ancestors would be happy and protected. (13) Linh helped place the food on a special table. (14) She made sure that everything looked perfect.

(15) At the temple, monks led the group in special prayers at the temple. (16) Linh didn't understand all the words, but she knew it was a way to show respect and love for her ancestors. (17) Linh lit candles placed in front of the altar. (18) She joined her family in their prayers.

(19) One of the most exciting moments for Linh was when they released paper lanterns into the night sky. (20) Each lantern carried a wish or a message to the ancestors. (21) Linh closed her eyes tightly and made a wish. (22) She wished for her grandparents to find happiness and peace in the afterlife.

(23) Le Vu Lan is not just about remembering the past. (24) It is also about making today's world a different place. (25) This festival is a time for good deeds. (26) Linh and her family donated food to those in need. (27) They reached out to help those who needed it. (28) Linh knew that they were making a change in the world. (29) That change was a positive one.

(30) Linh reflected on Le Vu Lan Bao Hieu. (31) She realized that it was a mix of beautiful traditions, family love, and being a good person. (32) It was a time when she felt deeply connected to her Vietnamese heritage and her family. (33) Linh has four cousins who live in the U.S.

(34) Linh respects her culture and the values that Le Vu Lan celebrates. (35) The festival is not just a one-day event. (36) It left a feeling in her heart. (37) It reminded her of the importance of family, the importance of tradition, and the importance of kindness.

PRACTICE #4 QUESTIONS

Which sentence would **BEST** follow and support sentence 3?

(1) Linh's eyes lit up as she heard that Le Vu Lan, the Vietnamese festival, had come once again. (2) She knew that this celebration was a time to remember and honor her ancestors, especially her grandparents who had lived in Vietnam. (3) Although she was born in America, Linh's family keeps their Vietnamese traditions.

A) Linh was born in the United States.
B) Another important celebration in Vietnamese culture is called Tet.
C) This festival held a special place in their hearts.
D) Linh went to bed early the night before so she would be well rested.

What is the **BEST** way to revise sentence 4?

(4) Like a big family reunion the festival was for Linh.

A) A big family reunion for Linh the festival was like.
B) For Linh a big family reunion the festival was like.
C) Was like the festival a big family reunion for Linh.
D) The festival was like a big family reunion for Linh.

The meaning of sentence 6 is unclear. What phrase should replace **things** in this sentence?

(6) The temple was beautifully decorated with things.

A) colorful lanterns and flowers
B) large crowds of people
C) much delicious food
D) many important traditions

Kyle needs a better topic sentence for the third paragraph (sentences 10-14). Which sentence should replace sentence 10?

(10) They did things to prepare. (11) There were spring rolls, steaming bowls of noodles, and many fresh fruits. (12) They believed that by offering these foods, their ancestors would be happy and protected. (13) Linh helped place the food on a special table. (14) She made sure that everything looked perfect.

A) There were so many things that Linh's family needed to do.
B) Linh's family worked hard to prepare delicious food for the ancestors.
C) Ancestors are people who lived before us and whom we are related to.
D) Spring Rolls are a light, crispy, and tender vegetarian food.

#5 Sentence 15 repeats information. In the box provided, rewrite sentence 15 in a clear and effective way.

(15) At the temple, monks led the group in special prayers at the temple.

____

____

____

#6 Which sentence would **BEST** follow and support sentence 20?

(19) One of the most exciting moments for Linh was when they released paper lanterns into the night sky. (20) Each lantern carried a wish or a message to the ancestors. (21) Linh closed her eyes tightly and made a wish. (22) She wished for her grandparents to find happiness and peace in the afterlife.

A) Linh thought the food looked so nice the way it was placed on the table.
B) Paper lanterns are also often used as decorations for weddings.
C) Watching the lanterns float away into the dark sky felt magical.
D) Paper lanterns come in many shapes and sizes.

#7 The meaning of sentence 24 is unclear. What word should replace **different** in this sentence?

(24) It was also about making today's world a [A) better / B) crowded / C) busy / D) excited] place.

A) better
B) crowded
C) busy
D) excited

What is the **BEST** way to combine sentences 28 and 29?

(28) Linh knew that they were making a change in the world. (29) That change was a positive one.

A) That change was a positive one that Linh knew they were making in the world.
B) Linh knew that they were making a positive change in the world.
C) Linh knew that they were making that change which was a positive one in the world.
D) In the world, they were making a positive change, and Linh knew that they were.

Kyle has included a sentence that does not belong in the seventh paragraph (sentences 30-33). Which sentence should he remove?

(30) Linh reflected on Le Vu Lan Bao Hieu. (31) She realized that it was a mix of beautiful traditions, family love, and being a good person. (32) It was a time when she felt deeply connected to her Vietnamese heritage and her family. (33) Linh has 4 cousins living in the U.S.

A) Sentence 30
B) Sentence 31
C) Sentence 32
D) Sentence 33

Sentence 37 repeats information. In the box provided, rewrite sentence 37 in a clear and effective way.

(37) It reminded her of the importance of family, the importance of tradition, and the importance of kindness.

____

____

____

REVISING: WARM-UP #5

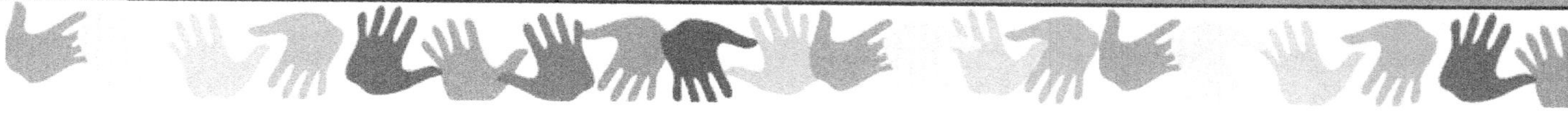

Sal wrote a story about a kid who made a change in his community. Read the story and see what revisions he should make. Then answer the questions that follow.

Positive Changes in the Park

(1) Tim loves to pick up trash in his neighborhood. (2) One day, he decided to ask his friends to join him in working in the local park. (3) They all said yes, and they started cleaning up the park every weekend. (4) People in the community saw what they were doing. (5) People thought it was a great idea.

(6) Because of Tim's decision to pick up trash and include his friends, more and more people in the neighborhood began helping too. (7) The park became better for everyone to enjoy. (8) People started to take better care of their neighborhood. (9) They even planted flowers. (10) They also added benches to make it even more beautiful. (11) Tim's mom loves flowers.

(12) All these positive changes happened because of Tim's small decision to clean up the park. (13) It inspired others to make their community better too. (14) A single choice can lead to positive changes in your community. (15) You can be the one to make a change!

#1 The meaning of sentence 2 is unclear. What phrase should replace **working in** from this sentence?

(2) One day, he decided to ask his friends to join him in the local park.

A) going to
B) cleaning up
C) playing at
D) hanging out in

#2 What is the **BEST** way to combine sentences 4 and 5?

(4) People in the community saw what they were doing. (5) People thought it was a great idea.

A) They saw what they were doing and thought it was a great idea the people in the community.
B) Because they thought it was a great idea, people in the community saw what they were doing.
C) People in the community saw what they were doing and thought it was a great idea.
D) It was a great idea thought the people in the community when they saw what they were doing.

The meaning of sentence 7 is unclear. What phrase should replace **<u>better</u>** in this sentence?

(7) The park became [A) large enough / B) more famous / C) less crowded / D) cleaner and safer] for everyone to enjoy.

A) large enough
B) more famous
C) less crowded
D) cleaner and safer

Sal has included a sentence that does not belong in the second paragraph (sentences 6-11). Which sentence should he remove?

(6) Because of Tim's decision to pick up trash and include his friends, more and more people in the neighborhood began helping too. (7) The park became better for everyone to enjoy. (8) People started to take better care of their neighborhood. (9) They even planted flowers. (10) They also added benches to make it even more beautiful. (11) Tim's mom loves flowers.

A) Sentence 8
B) Sentence 9
C) Sentence 10
D) Sentence 11

What is the **BEST** way to combine sentences 9 and 10?

(9) They even planted flowers. (10) They also added benches to make it even more beautiful.

____

____

REVISING: PRACTICE #5

Dalia wrote an essay with examples of community changes people can make. Read the essay and see what revisions she should make. Then answer the questions that follow.

Decide to Change Your Community

(1) People can do things in their communities. (2) Let's see what they are.

(3) One idea is cleaning up a park. (4) A group of friends decide to pick up trash in their local park. (5) They bring gloves and other things. (6) After a few weekends of cleaning, the park looks much nicer. (7) Families start visiting more often. (8) The community feels positive because of this group decision.

(9) There are also the trees. (10) These trees provide shade in the hot summer and make the town look beautiful. (11) Trees absorb pollution and remove it from the air. (12) Over time, more folks join in, and soon the whole town is covered in greenery over time.

(13) One family decides to start recycling at home. (14) They put their paper, plastic, and glass in separate bins. (15) Soon, their neighbors notice and decide to do the same.

(16) Creating a community garden is another option. (17) A group of neighbors gets together and creates a community garden. (18) They plant vegetables and flowers. (19) They share the food with others in the community, making everyone healthier.

(20) To improve traffic safety, the city council decides to put up stop signs at a dangerous intersection. (21) This decision keeps people safe because now everyone knows when to stop and go. (22) It's a simple change. (23) It makes a big difference in preventing accidents.

(24) Community members can work to support local businesses. (25) A group of friends decides to shop at small local stores instead of big chain stores. (26) This choice helps the local businesses stay open, and it keeps the money in the community, helping it grow.

(continued on next page)

REVISING: PRACTICE #5

Decide to Change Your Community (continued)

(27) Community events are the best! (28) They plan games, food, and music. (29) Many people come, and it brings the community closer together.

(30) Citizens can clean rivers. (31) A polluted river has been decided to be cleaned by a group of students and teachers. (32) They remove trash and work to keep the water clean. (33) As a result, fish return. (34) The river becomes a lovely place for everyone to enjoy.

(35) Neighbors help neighbors. (36) When a family in the community faces a tough time, everyone comes together to help. (37) It could be from a flood or it could be from a fire. (38) They bring food, clothes, and support. (39) This shows how helping one another can make a big difference in hard times.

(40) People decide to build a community center where everyone can be. (41) They have meetings, classes, and events there. (42) It becomes a center for learning and fun, making the community stronger.

(43) In these examples, individual or group decisions have a huge effect on the community. (44) Their actions can make our neighborhoods cleaner, safer, and more enjoyable. (45) Even small decisions can lead to big changes in our communities. (46) Each one of us can make a positive difference!

PRACTICE #5 QUESTIONS

Which sentences should replace sentences 1 and 2 to **BEST** state the central idea of this paper?

(1) People can do things in their communities. (2) Let's see what they are.

A) Decisions made by individuals or groups can make big changes to our communities. We'll explore some examples of positive community changes.
B) Often people share a common interest, which gives them a sense of community. Members of a community feel a sense of responsibility to one another.
C) There are different types of communities. Communities can be based on different things, like shared interests, geography, or identity.
D) Throughout history, groups of people have formed communities to increase their chances of survival. They may have shared an interest in providing food for their families, so they joined with others to hunt or farm.

The meaning of sentence 5 is unclear. What phrase should replace **other things** in this sentence?

(5) They bring gloves and

A) more items.
B) trash bags.
C) garbage to pick up.
D) healthy snacks.

Dalia needs a better topic sentence for the third paragraph (sentences 9-12). Which sentence should replace sentence 9?

(9) There are also the trees. (10) These trees provide shade in the hot summer and make the town look beautiful. (11) Trees absorb pollution and remove it from the air. (12) Over time, more folks join in, and soon the whole town is covered in greenery over time.

A) Some people decide to plant trees along the streets.
B) Trees provide homes to birds and squirrels.
C) What kid doesn't like climbing trees?
D) Gardens need lots of sun to support the crops.

Sentence 12 repeats information. In the box provided, rewrite sentence 12 in a clear and effective way.

(12) Over time, more folks join in, and soon the whole town is covered in greenery over time.

____

____

#5 Which sentence would **BEST** follow and support sentence 15?

(13) One family decides to start recycling at home. (14) They put their paper, plastic, and glass in separate bins. (15) Soon, their neighbors notice and decide to do the same.

A) Recycling can even be done at home.
B) Many people never take the time to recycle.
C) Some cities just don't have the money to have community recycling services.
D) This small choice helps reduce waste and pollution in their community.

#6 What is the **BEST** way to combine sentences 22 and 23?

(22) It's a simple change. (23) It makes a big difference in preventing accidents.

A) Because it makes a big difference in preventing accidents, it's a simple change.
B) It's a simple change, but it makes a big difference in preventing accidents.
C) It makes a simple difference that changes preventing big accidents.
D) When it makes a big difference in a simple change, it prevents accidents.

Dalia needs a better topic sentence for the eighth paragraph (sentences 27-29). Which sentence should replace sentence 27?

(27) Community events are the best! (28) They plan games, food, and music. (29) Many people come, and it brings the community closer together.

A) Although they may enjoy different types, most people enjoy listening to music.
B) There are many different ways that people can make changes in the community.
C) Some parents decide to organize a fun event in the neighborhood park.
D) A pickleball tournament is one example of a fun community event.

In the box provided, rewrite sentence 31 in a clear and effective way.

(31) A polluted river has been decided to be cleaned by a group of students and teachers.

What is the **BEST** way to combine sentences 36 and 37?

(36) When a family in the community faces a tough time, everyone comes together to help. (37) It could be from a flood or it could be from a fire.

A) When a family in the community faces a flood, or a fire, or some other kind of tough time, to help everyone else comes.
B) When a family in the community faces a tough time, like a flood or a fire, everyone comes together to help.
C) When everyone else comes to help when a flood, or a fire, or some other kind of tough time is faced by the community.
D) When a family in the community faces a tough time, everyone comes together to help, like a flood or a fire.

#10 The meaning of sentence 40 is unclear. What word should replace **be** in this sentence?

(40) People decide to build a community center where everyone can

A) exercise.
B) cook.
C) run.
D) gather.

REVISING: WARM-UP #6

Martin wrote this short essay to tell about Stonehenge. Read Martin's paper and look for revisions he should make. Then answer the questions that follow.

Mysterious Stonehenge and the Sun

(1) Stonehenge can be found in a field in England. (2) It is a huge circle of stones. (3) It stands in a field in England. (4) It's a mystery how the stones got there. (5) It's also a mystery why they are placed that way.

(6) On the summer solstice, the first official day of summer and the longest day of the year, something special happens. (7) The sun rises directly behind one of the tallest stones.

(8) There's a lot we don't understand. (9) We know that the people of Stonehenge knew a lot about the movement of the sun.
(10) Stonehenge is even believed to be aligned with the winter solstice. (11) Winter is by far my favorite season of them all.

#1 Read the first paragraph (sentences 1–5) again. Which sentence in this paragraph repeats information and should be removed?

(1) Stonehenge can be found in a field in England. (2) It is a huge circle of stones. (3) It stands in a field in England. (4) It's a mystery how the stones got there. (5) It's also a mystery why they are placed that way.

A) Sentence 2
B) Sentence 3
C) Sentence 4
D) Sentence 5

Which sentence would **BEST** follow and support sentence 7?

(6) On the summer solstice, the first official day of summer and the longest day of the year, something special happens. (7) The sun rises directly behind one of the tallest stones.

A) It looks like an orange fireball balancing on that tallest stone.
B) Earlier that morning the moon was also out.
C) That's the special thing that happens on that special day.
D) This event happens only on the first official day of summer.

Martin wants to combine the ideas in sentences 4 and 5. Write a new sentence that combines these ideas in a clear and effective way.

(4) It's a mystery how the stones got there. (5) It's also a mystery why they are placed that way.

____

____

The meaning of sentence 9 is unclear. Which word should replace **people** in this sentence?

(9) We know that the [A) drivers / B) authors / C) customers / D) builders] of Stonehenge knew a lot about the movement of the sun.

There is an extra sentence in paragraph 3 (sentences 8-11) that does not belong. Which sentence needs to be deleted?

(8) There's a lot we don't understand. (9) We know that the people of Stonehenge knew a lot about the movement of the sun. (10) It even is believed to be aligned with the winter solstice. (11) Winter is by far my favorite season of them all.

A) Sentence 8
B) Sentence 9
C) Sentence 10
D) Sentence 11

REVISING: PRACTICE #6

Holly read about communities in Social Studies. She wrote this paper to tell how communities respond to natural disasters. Read Holly's paper and look for revisions she needs to make. Then answer the questions that follow.

Gulf Coast Communities vs. Hurricanes

(1) Gulf Coast communities are interesting. (2) People are pulled to their beauty, resources, and climate. (3) Summers are usually hot. (4) Winters are mild. (5) In some Gulf Coast communities, fishing has been a way of life for hundreds of years. (6) Oil and natural gas businesses are also important. (7) Many communities offer beach homes and outdoor activities.

(8) There is something else the area is famous for: hurricanes. (9) Since 1900, more than 40 major hurricanes have hit states along the Gulf Coast. (10) Sometimes tornadoes strike the area as well. (11) Two recent hurricanes were very powerful. (12) In 2005, Hurricane Katrina crossed the southern tip of Florida and moved into the Gulf in 2005. (13) Then the storm turned north and grew stronger. (14) Finally, it hit the Louisiana and Mississippi coasts.

(15) In 2008, Hurricane Ike came ashore in Galveston, Texas. (16) Hurricanes start over the ocean. (17) The force of hurricane winds causes water to pile up ahead of the storm. (18) This is called a surge. (19) As the hurricane hits the coastline, this pile of water rushes over the land. (20) At first, the water level rises slowly. (21) As the eye of the storm moves closer, water rises quickly. (22) Next, heavy waves pound the coast.

(23) Hurricane Katrina's storm surge caused levees that protected the city of New Orleans to fail. (24) Much of the city and nearby areas were flooded. (25) Floods covered almost the entire city. (26) Entire neighborhoods were ruined. (27) Thousands of people were left homeless. (28) Many people died. (29) The storm surge from Hurricane Ike was 15 feet high when it hit Galveston Island. (30) Most houses along the beach were badly damaged or totally destroyed. (31) Power was knocked out over a wide area.

(32) When something bad happens, people do something. (33) Neighbors help neighbors. (34) The government also provides help as people return to the area. (35) The people can start to rebuild their homes. (36) They rebuild their businesses. (37) They also rebuild their lives.

(38) People who choose to live along the Gulf Coast know there's a chance their community may be hit by a powerful hurricane. (39) They do everything they can to prepare. (40) When a dangerous storm is approaching, most people leave and go to a different place. (41) After the storm has passed, they return home to all the benefits that come with living on the Gulf Coast after the storm has passed.

PRACTICE #6 QUESTIONS

Holly needs a topic sentence for the first paragraph (sentences 1-7). Which sentence should replace sentence 1?

(1) Gulf Coast communities are interesting.

A) Communities that border the Gulf Coast have a lot to offer.
B) Oil and gas are extremely important to our economy.
C) Outdoor activities include swimming, surfing, beach combing, and fishing.
D) The weather is nice most days.

The meaning of sentence 2 is unclear. Which phrase should replace **pulled to** in this sentence?

(2) People are pulled to the beauty, the resources, and the climate.

A) entered into
B) curious about
C) not interested in
D) attracted to

Holly has included a sentence that does not belong in the second paragraph (sentences 8-14). Which sentence should she remove?

(8) There is something else the area is famous for: hurricanes. (9) Since 1900, more than 40 major hurricanes have hit states along the Gulf Coast. (10) Sometimes tornadoes strike the area as well. (11) Two recent hurricanes were very powerful. (12) In 2005, Hurricane Katrina crossed the southern tip of Florida and moved into the Gulf in 2005. (13) Then the storm turned north and grew stronger. (14) Finally, it hit the Louisiana and Mississippi coasts.

A) Sentence 9
B) Sentence 10
C) Sentence 11
D) Sentence 12

#4

Sentence 12 repeats information and needs to be revised. In the box provided, rewrite sentence 12 in a clear and effective way.

(12) In 2005, Hurricane Katrina crossed the southern tip of Florida and moved into the Gulf in 2005.

____

____

Which sentence would **BEST** follow and support sentence 22?

(22) Next, heavy waves pound the coast. (23) Hurricane Katrina's storm surge caused levees that protected the city of New Orleans to fail.

A) Before the hurricane hits, things can be eerily calm.
B) After a few hours, the storm can pass.
C) Members of the community often crowd into stores to get supplies to help them through the hurricane.
D) A storm surge can knock down buildings, damage bridges and roads, and change the landscape.

Read the fourth paragraph (sentences 23-31) again. Which sentence in this paragraph repeats information and should be removed?

(23) Hurricane Katrina's storm surge caused levees that protected the city of New Orleans to fail. (24) Much of the city and nearby areas were flooded. (25) Floods covered almost the entire city. (26) Entire neighborhoods were ruined. (27) Thousands of people were left homeless. (28) Many people died. (29) The storm surge from Hurricane Ike was 15 feet high when it hit Galveston Island. (30) Most houses along the beach were badly damaged or totally destroyed. (31) Power was knocked out over a wide area.

A) Sentence 23
B) Sentence 25
C) Sentence 27
D) Sentence 29

Holly needs a better topic sentence for the sixth paragraph (sentences 32-37). Which sentence should replace sentence 32?

(32) When something bad happens, people do something.

A) While waiting for a hurricane to hit, time almost stands still.
B) Hurricanes can be weak or strong.
C) When a hurricane hits, communities work together to overcome the problems that follow.
D) People must be prepared before a hurricane hits.

#8 What is the **BEST** way to combine sentences 35, 36, and 37?

(35) The people can start to rebuild their homes. (36) They rebuild their businesses. (37) They also rebuild their lives.

A) When the people can start to rebuild their homes, they can rebuild their businesses and also their lives.
B) The people can start to rebuild their homes, their businesses, and their lives.
C) If the people can start to rebuild their homes, their businesses, and also their lives.
D) Because the people can start to rebuild their homes, they can rebuild their businesses and their lives.

The meaning of sentence 40 is unclear. Which word should replace **different** in this sentence?

(40) When a dangerous storm is approaching, most people leave and go to a

A) safer
B) nicer
C) nearby
D) expensive

place.

Sentence 41 repeats information and needs to be revised. In the box provided, rewrite sentence 41 in a clear and effective way.

(41) After the storm has passed, they return home to all the benefits that come with living on the Gulf Coast after the storm has passed.

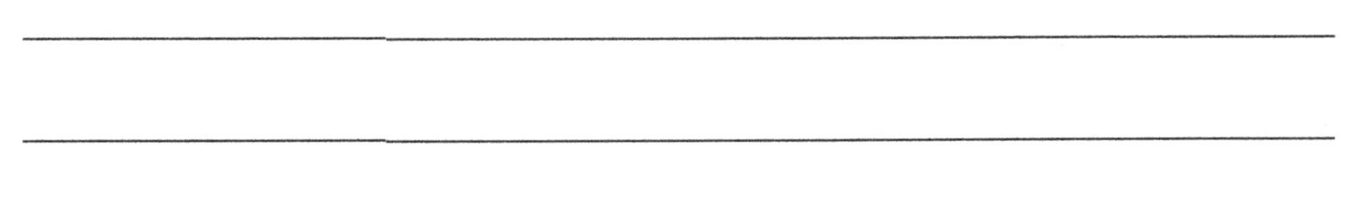

REVISING: WARM-UP #7

Sandra wrote a short essay about supply and demand. Read the essay and see what revisions she should make. Then answer the questions that follow.

Balancing Supply and Demand

(1) Supply and demand is like a seesaw that helps determine prices and how many items we can get. (2) Imagine supply as the amount of something available, like toys in a store. (3) When there are a lot of toys (high supply), prices usually stay lower because there are enough things for everyone. (4) But if there are only a few toys (low supply), prices can go up because they're harder to find, and there are only a few of them. (5) Squishmallow Stuffies are popular toys these days.

(6) Now, think about demand as how much the customers want those toys. (7) If everyone really wants the same toy, its price might go up because it's in high demand.

(8) You might notice something. (9) Each one affects the other. (10) If more people want a toy than there are toys available, the price goes up. (11) If there are lots of toys and not many people want them, the price goes down.

(12) So, supply and demand help decide what things cost and how much we can buy. (13) It's like a balancing act in the store!

The meaning of sentence 1 is unclear. What word should replace **get** in this sentence?

(1) Supply and demand is like a seesaw that helps determine prices and how many items we can get.

A) give
B) buy
C) make
D) deliver

The author has included a sentence that does not belong in the second paragraph (sentences 1-5). Which sentence should she remove?

(1) Supply and demand is like a seesaw that helps determine prices and how many items we can get. (2) Imagine supply as the amount of something available, like toys in a store. (3) When there are a lot of toys (high supply), prices usually stay lower because there's enough stuff for everyone. (4) But if there are only a few toys (low supply), prices can go up because they're harder to find, and there are only a few of them. (5) Squishmallow Stuffies are popular toys these days.

A) Sentence 2
B) Sentence 3
C) Sentence 4
D) Sentence 5

The meaning of sentence 3 is unclear. What word should replace **things** in this sentence?

(3) When there are a lot of toys (high supply) prices usually stay lower because there are enough [A) stuff / B) products / C) food / D) item] for everyone.

A) stuff
B) products
C) food
D) item

Which sentence would **BEST** follow and support sentence 7?

(6) Now, think about demand as how much the customers want those toys.
(7) If everyone really wants the same toy, its price might go up because it's in high demand.

A) But if a toy isn't very popular, its price might stay low.
B) Every year seems to bring a new popular toy.
C) Kids are happy to get these toys.
D) The stores are usually filled with excited shoppers.

The author needs a better topic sentence for the third paragraph (sentences 8-11). Which sentence should replace sentence 8?

(8) You might notice something. (9) Each one affects the other. (10) If more people want a toy than there are toys available, the price goes up. (11) If there are lots of toys and not many people want them, the price goes down.

A) The price goes up.
B) There are so many reasons for this.
C) Supply and demand are so interesting!
D) Supply and demand work together.

REVISING: PRACTICE #7

Megan wrote a story to show her understanding of supply and demand.
Read Megan's story and look for revisions she needs to make. Then answer the questions that follow.

Prairie Pearl's Popular Product

(1) Down in the big and bustling Lone Star State of Texas, there lived a clever cowgirl named Prairie Pearl. (2) Pearl was known far and wide for her special cowboy boots. (3) These boots were no ordinary boots; they were the comfiest and sturdiest boots anyone had ever worn.

(4) Now, one day, Pearl had an idea. (5) She said, "If I make more boots, I can sell them to more people, and they will all be happy!" (6) She worked extra hard. (7) She made many pairs of her magical boots. (8) When she took them to the market, she was so excited to see all the people who wanted to buy them.

(9) There were so many boots in the market that people didn't feel like they needed to buy them right away because there were so many boots in the market. (10) They said, "Well, Pearl has plenty of boots, so we can come back later." (11) Since everyone knew there were lots of boots, they didn't want to pay a high price for them.

(12) Pearl scratched her head and said, "What should I do now?" (13) She realized that she had made too many boots, and now there was more supply than demand. (14) That means there were too many boots and not enough people who wanted to buy them.

(15) Pearl did better. (16) And you know what? People started buying her boots again! (17) They loved getting such comfy boots, and they loved getting them at a lower price. (18) Pearl was happy because she was still selling her boots, and people were happy because they got a good deal.

(19) From that day on, Pearl learned an important lesson about supply and demand. (20) She realized that it's big to balance how much product you make with how much people want. (21) Sometimes, when there's too much of something, you might need to lower the price to make people interested. (22) And when there's not enough, you can raise the price a bit.

(23) Pearl kept making boots. (24) She made them correctly this time. (25) She always made sure to keep an eye on the supply and demand so everyone could have comfy boots at a real price. (26) And that's how Prairie Pearl's boots became famous not only for their comfort but also for their smart cowgirl maker who understood supply and demand very well.

PRACTICE #7 QUESTIONS

Which sentence would **BEST** follow and support sentence 3?

(3) These boots were no ordinary boots; they were the comfiest and sturdiest boots anyone had ever worn.

A) Pearl's boots were comfortable, strong, and very popular.
B) Pearl was born right here in Texas, the Lone Star State.
C) Everyone wanted a pair of Pearl's boots, and she could barely make them fast enough.
D) Many Texans like to wear cowboy boots, so that would be a good product to sell.

What is the **BEST** way to combine sentences 6 and 7?

(6) She worked extra hard. (7) She made many pairs of her magical boots.

A) She worked and made many pairs of her magical boots extra hard.
B) Even though she worked extra hard, she was still able to make many pairs of her magical boots.
C) She worked extra hard, or she also made many pairs of her magical boots.
D) She worked extra hard and made many pairs of her magical boots.

Megan wants to add a closing sentence to the second paragraph (sentences 4-8) to help transition to the next paragraph. Which sentence should she add after sentence 8?

(8) When she took them to the market, she was so excited to see all the people who wanted to buy them.

A) But something unexpected happened.
B) The people lined up to buy Pearl's boots.
C) This all happened when she took her boots to market.
D) Pearl thought she would go out of business.

Which sentence would BEST follow and support sentence 11?

(11) Since everyone knew there were lots of boots, they didn't want to pay a high price for them.

A) There were so many boots in the market.
B) Pearl always sold more boots in the winter.
C) People were more interested than ever in Pearl's boots.
D) So, they offered Pearl less money for her boots.

Which sentence would **BEST** follow and support sentence 14?

(14) That means there were too many boots and not enough people who wanted to buy them.

A) Pearl had no way of knowing this would happen because she didn't have much experience in business.
B) When there's too much of something and not enough people who want it, the price usually goes down.
C) Pearl had no choice other than to give away all of her boots and go back home.
D) This is what happens when people try new things without thinking them through.

Megan needs a better topic sentence for the fifth paragraph (sentences 15-18). Which sentence should replace sentence 15?

(15) Pearl did better. (16) And you know what? People started buying her boots again! (17) They loved getting such comfy boots, and they loved getting them at a lower price. (18) Pearl was happy because she was still selling her boots, and people were happy because they got a good deal.

A) Pearl had so many choices that she didn't know where to begin.
B) Pearl decided to lower the price of her boots a little to encourage people to buy them.
C) Pearl loved making boots and selling them to her customers.
D) People began to lose interest in Pearl's famous cowboy boots because they were so expensive.

Sentence 17 repeats information. In the box provided, rewrite sentence 17 in a clear and effective way.

(17) They loved getting such comfy boots, and they loved getting them at a lower price.

____

____

The meaning of sentence 20 is unclear. Which word should replace **big** to make sentence 20 more clear?

(20) She realized that it's

A) important
B) large
C) unwise
D) confusing

to balance how much product you make with how much people want.

Megan needs a better topic sentence for the seventh paragraph (sentences 23-26). Which sentence should replace sentences 23 and 24?

(23) Pearl kept making boots. (24) She made them correctly this time.

A) Pearl learned new and better ways to make her cowboy boots better than ever.
B) I hope you enjoyed my story about Prairie Pearl as much as I enjoyed writing it!
C) Pearl continued to make her special boots, but this time, she made just the right amount.
D) Business was booming, and Pearl decided to start making cowboy hats too.

The meaning of sentence 25 is unclear. Which word should replace **real** to make sentence 25 more clear?

(25) She always made sure to keep an eye on the supply and demand, so everyone could have comfy boots at a real price.

A) expensive
B) fair
C) cheap
D) low

Part 2: Editing

Editing Strategies:

- ☑ **Highlight the key words in the question.**
- ☑ **Highlight the sentence or paragraph in the passage.**
- ☑ **Read the sentence/paragraph out loud (or use a whisper phone).**
- ☑ **Try each answer choice.**
- ☑ **Eliminate/cross out answers that do not make sense.**
- ☑ **Choose the answer that makes the most sense.**
- ☑ **Lastly, justify your answer!**

Revise	Edit
ARMS	CUPS
A — Add sentences and words.	**C** — Capitals: sentences, names, places, months, titles, I
R — Remove words or sentences.	**U** — Usage: match nouns and verbs correctly, grammar usage
M — Move a word or sentence.	**P** — Punctuation: . ! ? ' , " "
S — Substitute words or sentences.	**S** — Spelling: Check all words, use your resources.

What is EDITING?

- Editing is the process of ensuring the **correctness** of your writing. Is it **correct** or not?
- Editing is capitalization, usage of grammar, punctuation, and spelling!
- Editing is **reviewing** and **fixing** your conventions so that people can understand it!

EDITING: WARM-UP #1

Max is writing a story about someone who improved their community. Read this paragraph from the body of Max's story and look for corrections he needs to make. Then answer the questions that follow.

Big Change

(1) Sue noticed her neighborhood park was littered and dull. (2) She wants to make a change. (3) She gathered her friends and organized a cleanup day. (4) They collected trash painted benches, and planted flowers. (5) Sue also set up a "Little Library" where kid's could exchange books. (6) The park changed into a lively place of laughter and learning. (7) Because for her efforts, neighbors began holding regular events. (8) Sue's small actions sparked a positive change. (9) Proved that even the littlest hands can make a big difference.

#1 What change should be made in sentence 2?

(2) She wants to make a change.

A) Change **wants** to **wanted**
B) Change **make** to **makes**
C) Change **change** to **changes**
D) Change the period to a question mark

What change should be made in sentence 4?

(4) They collected trash painted benches, and planted flowers.

A) Change **They** to **Them**
B) Change **collected** to **collecting**
C) Insert a comma after **trash**
D) Change **flowers** to **Flowers**

What change should be made in sentence 5?

(5) Sue also set up a "Little Library" where kid's could exchange books.

A) Change **up** to **in**
B) Change **where** to **when**
C) Change **kid's** to **kids**
D) Change **could** to **couldn't**

#4 What change should be made in sentence 7?

(7) Because for her efforts, neighbors began holding regular events.

A) Change **for** to **of**
B) Change **efforts** to **efferts**
C) Change **began** to **begin**
D) Change **events** to **Events**

Sentence 9 is written incorrectly. Select the **ONE** response that corrects this sentence.

(9) [A) And proved. That / B) This proved that / C) Learning about that / D) This proved it. That] even the littlest hands can make a big difference.

EDITING: PRACTICE #1A

Hiram is writing a paper that identifies the characteristics of citizenship. Read the first paragraph of Hiram's paper and look for corrections he needs to make. Then answer the questions that follow.

Citizenship

(1) Good citizenship means being responsible respectful, and empathetic. (2) Responsible citizens follows laws, pay taxes, and vote. (3) Respect for others creates a positive community. (4) Empathy leads to acts for kindness and aid for those in need. (5) Good citizens support the environment by reducing waste. (6) They perform community service. (7) Volunteer their time. (8) By supported justice and equality, good citizens support fairness. (9) These characteristics create a strong society.

#1 What change should be made in sentence 1?

(1) Good citizenship means being responsible respectful, and empathetic.

A) Change **means** to **mean**
B) Change **being** to **was being**
C) Insert a comma after **responsible**
D) Change **respectful** to **respectfull**

What change should be made in sentence 2?

(2) Responsible citizens follows laws, pay taxes, and vote.

A) Change **follows** to **follow**
B) Change **pay** to **paying**
C) Change **and** to **also**
D) Change **vote** to **voting**

What change should be made in sentence 4?

(4) Empathy leads to acts for kindness and aid for those in need.

A) Change **leads** to **led**
B) Change **acts** to **act's**
C) Change **for** to **of**
D) Change **aid** to **ade**

#4 Sentence 7 is written incorrectly. Select the **ONE** response that corrects this sentence.

(7) [A) And also. They / B) They also / C) Doing that they / D) They do it, they] volunteer their time.

#5 What change should be made in sentence 8?

(8) By supported justice and equality, good citizens support fairness.

A) Change **By** to **To**
B) Change **supported** to **supporting**
C) Change **good** to **best**
D) Change **fairness** to **fareness**

EDITING: PRACTICE #1B

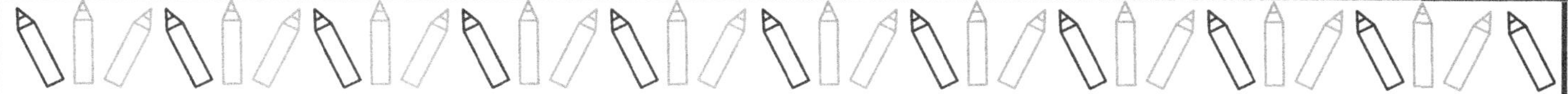

Laura is writing a paper about someone she considers an American hero. Read these three paragraphs from the body of Laura's paper and look for corrections she needs to make. Then answer the questions that follow.

Helen Keller

(1) Helen Keller was an amazing person. (2) She showed that you can do anything, no matter what challenges you face. (3) She was born on June 27, 1880, in alabama. (4) Helen became very sick when she was just 19 months old. (5) This illness left her unable to see or here. (6) Even though it was hard, Helen didn't give up.

(7) When she was seven years old, a wonderful teacher named Anne Sullivan came to help her. (8) Anne teached Helen how to read and write. (9) She used a special method where words were spelled into her hand. (10) Helen learned so quickly that she went to College and became the first deaf-blind person to earn a degree.

(11) Helen traveled around the world. (12) And gave speeches and wrote books to inspire others. (13) She showed that with determination, you can achieve great things. (14) Helen Keller will always be remembered as a hero and a symbol of courage.

#1 What change should be made in sentence 3?

(3) She was born on June 27, 1880, in alabama.

A) Change **She** to **Her**
B) Change **born** to **borned**
C) Change **June** to **june**
D) Change **alabama** to **Alabama**

What change should be made in sentence 5?

(5) This illness left her unable to see or here.

A) Change **illness** to **Illness**
B) Change **unable** to **unabel**
C) Change **see** to **sea**
D) Change **here** to **hear**

What change should be made in sentence 8?

(8) Anne teached Helen how to read and write.

A) Change **teached** to **taught**
B) Change **how** to **why**
C) Change **and** to **or**
D) Change **write** to **right**

What change should be made in sentence 10?

(10) Helen learned so quickly that she went to College and became the first deaf-blind person to earn a degree.

A) Change **quickly** to **quick**
B) Change **went** to **goes**
C) Change **College** to **college**
D) Change **earn** to **earned**

Sentence 12 is written incorrectly. Select the **ONE** response that corrects this sentence.

(12) [A) And gave speeches. And / B) Giving speeches and / C) She gave speeches and / D) She gave them, she] wrote books to inspire others.

EDITING: WARM-UP #2

Max is writing a story about someone who improved their community. Read this paragraph from the body of Max's story and look for corrections he needs to make. Then answer the questions that follow.

Daniel Boone's Community

(1) Daniel Boone was a brave explorer who helped create a town called Boonesborough in kentucky. (2) In 1775, Daniel led a group of settlers for the wilderness. (3) They traveled a long way on a trail called the Wilderness Road. (4) Daniel helped clear this road.

(5) They reached a good spot by the Kentucky River they built a fort to keep everyone safe. (6) They named it Boonesborough after Daniel Boone.
(7) The fort was made of strong wooden walls to protect the settlers from wild animals and other dangers.

(8) Boonesborough became one of the first towns in Kentucky. (9) Daniel and the settlers worked hard to build houses plant crops, and make friends with the Native Americans. (10) Life was tough, but Daniel's courage and leadership helped the town grow.

(11) Daniel Boone is remembered as a pioneer who helped explore and settle new land. (12) He makes it safe for many families to live and thrive.

What change should be made in sentence 1?

(1) Daniel Boone was a brave explorer who helped create a town called Boonesborough in kentucky.

A) Change **was** to **were**
B) Change **explorer** to **explorers**
C) Change **who** to **he**
D) Change **kentucky** to **Kentucky**

#2 Sentence 2 is written incorrectly. Select the ONE response that corrects this sentence.

(2) In 1775, Daniel led a group of settlers [A) over / B) with / C) through / D) on] the wilderness.

A) over
B) with
C) through
D) on

What is the correct way to write sentence 5?

(5) They reached a good spot by the Kentucky River they built a fort to keep everyone safe.

A) They reached a good spot by the Kentucky River and built a fort to keep everyone safe.
B) They reached a good spot by the Kentucky River. Building a fort to keep everyone safe.
C) They reached a good spot by the Kentucky River and built it to keep everyone safe. A fort.
D) They reached a good spot by the Kentucky River. And built a fort to keep everyone safe.

#4 What change should be made in sentence 9?

(9) Daniel and the settlers worked hard to build houses plant crops, and make friends with the Native Americans.

A) Change **settlers** to **settler**
B) Insert a comma after **houses**
C) Change **friends** to **friend's**
D) Change **with** to **from**

#5 What change should be made in sentence 12?

(12) He makes it safe for many families to live and thrive.

A) Change **makes** to **made**
B) Change **for** to **four**
C) Change **families** to **familys**
D) Change **thrive** to **thriving**

EDITING: PRACTICE #2A

Georgia is writing a paper comparing light and sound energy. Read these two paragraphs from the body of Georgia's paper and look for corrections she needs to make. Then answer the questions that follow.

Light and Sound

(1) First, we'll talk about light. (2) Light is a form of energy we can see. (3) It travels in waves. (4) It's just like the ripples you see when you throw a stone over a pond. (5) Light waves can travel through space. (6) This is why we can see the sun and stars even though they are very far away. (7) Light travels very fast at about 186,000 miles per second! (8) That is why en entire room lights up instantly after turning on the lights. (9) Light can come from many sources, like the sun, light bulbs, and even fireflys.

(10) Now, let's look at sound. (11) Sound is also a type of energy it travels in waves. (12) When you clap your hands, you create sound waves that travel through the air to your ears. (13) This allows you to hear the clap. (14) Sound cant travel through the empty space of outer space. (15) This is because there is no air or other material to carry the sound waves. (16) Sound travels much slowly than light.

#1 Georgia has made an error in sentence 4. Select the ONE response that corrects this error.

(4) It's just like the ripples you see when you throw a

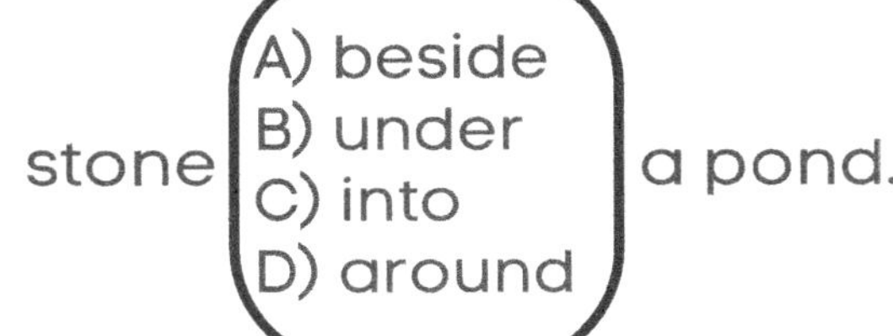

stone
A) beside
B) under
C) into
D) around
a pond.

What change should be made in sentence 9?

(9) Light can come from many sources, like the sun, light bulbs, and even fireflys.

A) Change **come** to **comes**
B) Change **sources** to **source**
C) Remove the comma after **sun**
D) Change **fireflys** to **fireflies**

What is the correct way to write sentence 11?

(11) Sound is also a type of energy it travels in waves.

A) Sound is also a type of energy, and it travels. In waves.
B) Sound is also a type of energy that travels in waves.
C) Sound is also a type of energy, it travels in waves.
D) Sound is also a type of energy. And it travels in waves.

What change should be made in sentence 14?

(14) Sound cant travel through the empty space of outer space.

A) Change **cant** to **can't**
B) Change **travel** to **travle**
C) Change **through** to **under**
D) Change **outer space** to **Outer Space**

What change should be made in sentence 16?

(16) Sound travels much slowly than light.

A) Change **travels** to **travel's**
B) Insert **too** after **travels**
C) Change **slowly** to **slower**
D) Change **light** to **lightest**

EDITING: PRACTICE #2B

Sophie is writing a paper for her science class. Read these three paragraphs from the body of Sophie's paper and look for corrections she needs to make. Then answer the questions that follow.

Solids, Liquids, and Gases

(1) Solids are materials that keep their shape no matter where you put them. (2) Think about your school desk, a rock, or an ice cube. (3) These objects dont change shape when you move them around. (4) All matter is made of tiny particles, and in solids, these particles are called molecules. (5) They are packed tightly together and don't move much. (6) This is why solids are firm and hold there shape.

(7) Liquids are materials that can flow and take the shape of the container they are in. (8) Water juice, and milk are all examples of liquids. (9) If you pour water into a cup, it takes the shape of the cup. (10) The molecules in liquids are not as tightly packed as in solids. (11) They can move around more freely, allowing liquids to flow and change shape easy.

(12) Gases are materials that spread out to fill any space they are in. (13) The air we breathe, the helium in balloons, and the steam from a boiling pot of water are all examples of gases. (14) The molecules in gases are spread out they move around quickly in all directions. (15) Because of this, gases can expand to fill any container, no matter the size.

What change should be made in sentence 3?

(3) These objects dont change shape when you move them around.

A) Change **these** to **this**
B) Change **dont** to **don't**
C) Change **move** to **moves**
D) Change **them** to **it**

What change should be made in sentence 6?

(6) This is why solids are firm and hold there shape.

A) Change **solids** to **Solids**
B) Change **are** to **is**
C) Insert a comma after **firm**
D) Change **there** to **their**

What change should be made in sentence 8?

(8) Water juice, and milk are all examples of liquids.

A) Insert a comma after **Water**
B) Change **milk** to **Milk**
C) Change **are** to **is**
D) Change **examples** to **example**

Sentence 11 is written incorrectly. Select the **ONE** response that corrects this sentence.

(11) They can move around more freely, allowing liquids to flow and change shape

A) more easier.
B) easiest.
C) easily.
D) most easy.

What is the correct way to write sentence 14?

(14) The molecules in gases are spread out they move around quickly in all directions.

A) The molecules in gases are spread out, and they move around quickly. In all directions.
B) The molecules in gases are spread out and move around quickly in all directions.
C) The molecules in gases are spread out, they move around quickly in all directions.
D) The molecules in gases are spread out. And they move around quickly in all directions.

EDITING: WARM-UP #3

Dana is writing a paper for her science class. Read these four paragraphs from the body of Dana's paper and look for corrections she needs to make. Then answer the questions that follow.

The Food Chain

(1) The son is the main source of energy for everything on Earth. (2) Plants use sunlight to make their food through a process called photosynthesis. (3) This makes plants producers because they produce their own food. (4) Imagine green grass beside a field soaking up sunlight.

(5) Many animals eat plants. (6) Called herbivores. (7) A rabbit munching on the grass is a good example. (8) The rabbit gets energy from the grass it eats. (9) This makes the rabbit a primary consumer because it is the first animal in the food chain that eats a producer.

(10) There is animals that eat other animals. (11) These animals are called carnivores. (12) A fox that eats the rabbit is a good example of this. (13) The fox gets energy from the rabbit. (14) This makes it a secondary consumer because it is the second animal in the chain.

(15) When plants and animals die, decomposers like bacteria break down their bodys. (16) This returns nutrients to the soil and helps new plants grow.

What change should be made in sentence 1?

(1) The son is the main source of energy for everything on Earth.

A) Change **son** to **sun**
B) Change **is** to **are**
C) Change **energy** to **Energy**
D) Change **everything** to **every thing**

#2 Dana has made an error in sentence 4. Select the **ONE** response that corrects this error.

(4) Imagine green grass [A) near / B) above / C) in / D) toward] a field soaking up sunlight.

A) near
B) above
C) in
D) toward

#3 Dana has made an error in sentence 6. Select the **ONE** response that corrects this error.

(6) [A) Calling those animals / B) And they. Are called / C) It is called / D) They are called] herbivores.

A) Calling those animals
B) And they. Are called
C) It is called
D) They are called

#4 What change should be made in sentence 10?

(10) There is animals that eat other animals.

A) Change **is** to **are**
B) Change **animals** to **animal's**
C) Change **eat** to **ate**
D) Change **other** to **another**

#5 What change should be made in sentence 15?

(15) When plants and animals die, decomposers like bacteria break down their bodys.

A) Change **plants** to **plant's**
B) Change **animals** to **animels**
C) Change **their** to **there**
D) Change **bodys** to **bodies**

EDITING: PRACTICE #3A

Alan is writing a persuasive essay in favor of creating a budget. Read these two paragraphs from the opening of Alan's paper and look for corrections he needs to make. Then answer the questions that follow.

Creating a Budget

(1) Imagine you have a piggy bank where you keep all your money. (2) Wouldn't it be great to make sure you have enough money for the things you want to buy. (3) This is where a simple budget comes in. (4) Creating a budget helps you decide how to spend and save your money wise. (5) Let's see why it's a good idea.

(6) First, a budget helps you plan your spending. (7) Imagine you get $10 a week for allowance. (8) With out a budget, you might spend all your money on candy and toys right away. (9) But what if you want to buy a cool video game that costs $40? (10) If you spend all your money on small things, you won't have enough for the game. (11) A budget help you decide how much to spend on fun things now and how much to save for bigger things later. (12) You might decide to spend $5 on treats and save $5 each week. (13) For just eight weeks, you'll have enough for that video game!

What change should be made in sentence 2?

(2) Wouldn't it be great to make sure you have enough money for the things you want to buy.

A) Change **Wouldn't** to **Wouldnt**
B) Change **make** to **made**
C) Change **buy** to **by**
D) Change the period to a question mark

Alan has made an error in sentence 4. Select the **ONE** response that corrects this error.

(4) Creating a budget helps you decide how to spend and save your money

A) wisely.
B) wiser.
C) wisest.
D) more wiser.

What change should be made in sentence 8?

(8) With out a budget, you might spend all your money on candy and toys right away.

A) Change **With out** to **Without**
B) Change **spend** to **spent**
C) Change **on** to **by**
D) Change **toys** to **toy's**

What change should be made in sentence 11?

(11) A budget help you decide how much to spend on fun things now and how much to save for bigger things later.

A) Change **budget** to **Budget**
B) Change **help** to **helps**
C) Change **spend** to **spent**
D) Change **bigger** to **more bigger**

Alan has made an error in sentence 13. Select the **ONE** response that corrects this error.

(13)

A) With
B) Into
C) In
D) Since

just eight weeks, you'll have enough for that video game!

EDITING: PRACTICE #3B

Olivia is writing an essay on the effects of pollution on the environment. Read these three paragraphs from the body of Olivia's paper and look for corrections she needs to make. Then answer the questions that follow.

Effects of Pollution

(1) One problem is water pollution. (2) Some factorys dump waste into rivers. (3) This can make the water dirty and unsafe for animals and plants. (4) Imagine a river filled with colorful fish and green plants. (5) If pollution enters the river, it can kill the fish and make the water look murky and gross. (6) The once-beautiful river can turn into a lifeless, dirty stream.

(7) Another kind of pollution is air pollution. (8) Factories and cars release smoke and harmful gases on the air. (9) This pollution can create smog, which is a thick, dirty fog that makes it hard to see and breathe. (10) In cities with lots of air pollution, the sky can look gray instead of blew. (11) Plants and buildings can get covered in a layer of grime. (12) This changes how the city looks and can making it a less pleasant place to live.

(13) Finally, let's think about land pollution. (14) When people litter or dump garbage in forests and parks, it can harm the soil and plants. (15) Animals might eat the trash and get sick. (16) Plants might not grow as well. (17) Over time, a beutiful forest could become a polluted area with with sick animals and fewer trees.

What change should be made in sentence 2?

(2) Some factorys dump waste into rivers.

A) Change **factorys** to **factories**
B) Change **dumped** to **dumping**
C) Change **waste** to **waist**
D) Change **rivers** to **Rivers**

Olivia has made an error in sentence 8. Select the **ONE** response that corrects this error.

(8) Factories and cars release smoke and harmful gases

A) over
B) up
C) into
D) near

the air.

What change should be made in sentence 10?

(10) In cities with lots of air pollution, the sky can look gray instead of blew.

A) Change **cities** to **citys**
B) Change **sky** to **Sky**
C) Change **look** to **looked**
D) Change **blew** to **blue**

#4

What change should be made in sentence 12?

(12) This changes how the city looks and can making it a less pleasant place to live.

A) Change **changes** to **changing**
B) Change **city** to **cities**
C) Change **making** to **make**
D) Change **live** to **life**

Olivia has made an error in sentence 17. Select the **ONE** response that corrects this error.

(17) Over time, a

A) beatiful
B) beautiful
C) beautyful
D) beautifull

forest could become a polluted area with with sick animals and fewer trees.

EDITING: WARM-UP #4

Wendy is writing a paper for her science class. Read these four paragraphs from the body of Wendy's paper and look for corrections she needs to make. Then answer the questions that follow.

Sam's Wagon

(1) Sam placed a few toys in the wagon and gave it a gentel push. (2) The wagon rolled smoothly forward on the grass. (3) "Wow, it's moving!" Sam exclaimed. (4) He was fascinated by how a little push could set the wagon in motion. (5) Sam noticed that the more harder he pushed, the faster the wagon went.

(6) Sam decided to try pulling the wagon, so he grabed the handle. (7) He walked backwards, and the wagon followed along. (8) This helped Sam understand that pulling could also change the wagons position and motion. (9) "Pulling is just as important as pushing," Sam thought. (10) Then, Sam had an idea. (11) "What if I try to change its direction?" Sam wondered.

(12) He gived the handle a sharp tug to the left, and the wagon turned left. (13) Pulling it to the right made the wagon change direction again. (14) Sam was excited to see how easily the wagon's path could be changed by pulling it in different directions.

#1 What change should be made in sentence 1?

(1) Sam placed a few toys in the wagon and gave it a gentel push.

A) Change **toys** to **toy's**
B) Change **wagon** to **Wagon**
C) Insert a comma after **wagon**
D) Change **gentel** to **gentle**

What change should be made in sentence 5?

(5) Sam noticed that the more harder he pushed, the faster the wagon went.

A) Change **noticed** to **noticing**
B) Change **more harder** to **harder**
C) Change **faster** to **fastest**
D) Change **went** to **go**

What change should be made in sentence 6?

(6) Sam decided to try pulling the wagon, so he grabed the handle.

A) Change **try** to **tried**
B) Change **decided** to **decides**
C) Delete the comma after **wagon**
D) Change **grabed** to **grabbed**

#4 What change should be made in sentence 8?

(8) This helped Sam understand that pulling could also change the wagons position and motion.

A) Change **helped** to **was helping**
B) Change **understand** to **under stand**
C) Change **pulling** to **puling**
D) Change **wagons** to **wagon's**

Wendy has made an error in sentence 12. Select the **ONE** response that corrects this error.

(12) He [A) given / B) was giving / C) gave / D) had given] the handle a sharp tug to the left, and the wagon turned left.

EDITING: PRACTICE #4A

Terrance is writing a paper for science class. Read the first four paragraphs from his paper and look for corrections he needs to make. Then answer the questions that follow.

Natural Resources in Clothing

(1) Natural resources are materials we get from nature, and they are very important for making clothes. (2) Let's explore some of these materials and why they are great for making what we where.

(3) First, there's cotton. (4) Cotton comes from plants and is soft and breathable. (5) This means cotton clothes felt nice on your skin and help you stay cool. (6) Cotton can also soak up sweat, keeping you dry. (7) That's why T-shirts and jeans are often made from cotton.

(8) Wool comes from sheep. (9) It is known for being warm. (10) Wool traps heat. (11) This makes it perfect for winter clothes like sweaters and hats. (12) Wool is also good at keeping you dry because it doesnt soak up water easily. (13) Even if it rains, wool can help you stay warm.

(14) Linen comes from the flax plant. (15) Linen is strong and can absorb a lot of moisture, making it gooder for hot weather. (16) Linen clothes are cool and comfortable, and they let your skin breathe. (17) Linen also has a unique texture that looks and feels speshel.

What change should be made in sentence 2?

(2) Let's explore some of these materials and why they are great for making what we where.

A) Change **Let's** to **Lets**
B) Change **materials** to **material's**
C) Change **are** to **is**
D) Change **where** to **wear**

#2 Terrance has made an error in sentence 5. Select the **ONE** response that corrects this error.

(5) This means cotton clothes [A) feel / B) had felt / C) feeling / D) were feeling] nice on your skin and help you stay cool.

A) feel
B) had felt
C) feeling
D) were feeling

#3 What change should be made in sentence 12?

(12) Wool is also good at keeping you dry because it doesnt soak up water easily.

A) Change **keeping** to **kept**
B) Change **doesnt** to **doesn't**
C) Insert a comma after **water**
D) Change **easily** to **easy**

#4 Terrance has made an error in sentence 15. Select the **ONE** response that corrects this error.

(15) Linen is strong and can absorb a lot of moisture, making it [A) most best / B) more better / C) better / D) most good] for hot weather.

A) most best
B) more better
C) better
D) most good

#5 What change should be made in sentence 17?

(17) Linen also has a unique texture that looks and feels speshel.

A) Change **has** to **have**
B) Change **texture** to **Texture**
C) Change **looks** to **look**
D) Change **speshel** to **special**

EDITING: PRACTICE #4B

Dale is writing a paper for social studies. Read the first four paragraphs from his paper and look for corrections he needs to make. Then answer the questions that follow.

The Picnic

(1) Mia loved playing with her friends and exploring the countryside. (2) One day, she and her friends decided to have a picnic by the river. (3) They bringed sandwiches, apples, cookies, and a big bottle of lemonade.

(4) When they arrived at their favorite spot, they laid out the food and began to eat. (5) But soon, they noticed a problem. (6) There were only four cookies, but there were six friends. (7) This was an example of scarcity. (8) Scarcity means there isn't enuff of something for everyone. (9) They realized they had to figure out a fair way to share the cookies so everyone could have a taste.

(10) While they were thinking, Mia's friend Ben said, "Why don't we break each cookie in half?" (11) Everyone agreed, and they divided the cookies into more smaller pieces. (12) Everyone got a share. (13) They learned that sometimes you have to find creative solutions when there's not enough of something.

(14) When it was time to go home, they realized only a few drops of lemonade were left in the bottel. (15) Everyone was thirsty. (16) This was another example of scarcity. (17) Mia had a great idea. (18) She found an extra water bottle at the bottom of her bag, and she mixed it with the lemonade to make it last longer. (19) It wasn't as sweet, but it was enough to quench there thirst.

#1 Dale has made an error in sentence 3. Select the **ONE** response that corrects this error.

(3) They [A) brought / B) was bringing / C) bring / D) are bringing] sandwiches, apples, cookies, and a big bottle of lemonade.

- A) brought
- B) was bringing
- C) bring
- D) are bringing

What change should be made in sentence 8?

(8) Scarcity means there isn't enuff of something for everyone.

A) Change **there** to **they're**
B) Change **wasn't** to **wasnt**
C) Change **enuff** to **enough**
D) Insert a comma after **something**

What change should be made in sentence 11?

(11) Everyone agreed, and they divided the cookies into more smaller pieces.

A) Change **Everyone** to **Every one**
B) Change **cookies** to **cookie's**
C) Change **more smaller** to **smaller**
D) Change **smaller** to **smallest**

#4 What change should be made in sentence 14?

(14) When it was time to go home, they realized only a few drops of lemonade were left in the bottel.

A) Change **go** to **went**
B) Change **they** to **them**
C) Change **drops** to **drop**
D) Change **bottel** to **bottle**

#5 What change should be made in sentence 19?

(19) It wasn't as sweet, but it was enough to quench there thirst.

A) Change **wasn't** to **weren't**
B) Change **sweet** to **sweets**
C) Remove the comma after **sweet**
D) Change **there** to **their**

EDITING: WARM-UP #5

Cindy is writing a paper for her science class. Read these paragraphs from the body of Cindy's paper and look for corrections she needs to make. Then answer the questions that follow.

The Sun

(1) The Sun is a star, just like the tiny dots of light you see in the night sky. (2) It is much closer to us than any other star. (3) This is why it looks so much big and bright. (4) The light and warmth from the Sun travel through space to reach us. (5) The Sun is so far away that this light takes about eight minutes to get here!

(6) The Sun gives us both light and thermal energy. (7) Light energy from the Sun makes our days bright. (8) It helps plants through a process called photosynthesis to make their own food. (9) Without sunlight, plants won't grow, and we won't have food to eat.

(10) Thermal energy from the Sun is what makes us feel warm. (11) When you stand outside on a sunny day, you can feel the heat from the Sun on your skin. (12) This heat is very important because it keeps our planet warm enough for people animals, and plants to live. (13) With out the Sun's heat, Earth would be a cold and dark place.

(14) The Sun also helps to create weather patterns. (15) The heat from the Sun warm up the air and water on Earth. (16) These movements help spread heat around the planet. (17) This makes different climates and weather patterns.

Cindy has made an error in sentence 3. Select the **ONE** response that corrects this error.

(3) This is why it looks so much

A) biggest and brightest.
B) more bigger and brighter.
C) bigger and brighter.
D) most big and bright.

What is the correct way to write sentence 8?

(8) It helps through a process called photosynthesis to make their own food.

A) It helps plants make their own food. Through a process called photosynthesis.
B) It helps plants make their own food through a process called photosynthesis.
C) It helps plants through a process called photosynthesis, to make their own food.
D) It helps plants through a process called photosynthesis. To make their own food.

What change should be made in sentence 12?

(12) This heat is very important because it keeps our planet warm enough for people animals, and plants to live.

A) Change **is** to **are**
B) Change **keeps** to **kept**
C) Insert a comma after **people**
D) Change **live** to **lived**

What change should be made in sentence 13?

(13) With out the Sun's heat, Earth would be a cold and dark place.

A) Change **With out** to **Without**
B) Change **Sun's** to **Suns**
C) Insert a comma after **cold**
D) Change **dark** to **darkest**

What change should be made in sentence 15?

(15) The heat from the Sun warm up the air and water on Earth.

A) Change **from** to **to**
B) Change **warm** to **warms**
C) Change **on** to **inside**
D) Change the **period** to a **question mark**

EDITING: PRACTICE #5A

Julia is writing a paper for her science class. Read these paragraphs from the body of Julia's paper and look for corrections she needs to make. Then answer the questions that follow.

Sound Energy

(1) Music is a fantastic example of sound energy. (2) When you listen to your favorite songs on the radio or through headphones, the sound waves travel from the speakers to your ears. (3) This might make you want to dance or sing along. (4) Musical instruments like guitars pianos, and drums create sound energy.

(5) Have you ever heard a dog bark or a bird sing. (6) Animals use sound energy to communicate too. (7) Dogs bark to warn you of danger or to say hello. (8) Birds is singing to attract mates or mark their territory. (9) These sounds help animals survive and interact with their environment.

(10) When you watch TV or play video games, sound energy makes the experience more better. (11) The voices of characters, the background music, and the special effects all come to life through sound. (12) Imagine watching a movie without any sound. (13) It wouldn't be as fun!

(14) Finally, think about emergency sirens, like those on fire trucks or ambulances. (15) These loud sounds use sound energy to warn people this helps keep them safe. (16) When you hear a siren, you know to be careful and make way for the emergency vehicle.

What change should be made in sentence 4?

(4) Musical instruments like guitars pianos, and drums create sound energy.

A) Change **instruments** to **instrument**
B) Insert a comma after **guitars**
C) Change **create** to **created**
D) Change **sound energy** to **Sound Energy**

What change should be made in sentence 5?

(5) Have you ever heard a dog bark or a bird sing.

A) Change **heard** to **hurd**
B) Change **bark** to **barks**
C) Change **sing** to **sang**
D) Change the period to a question mark

Julia has made an error in sentence 8. Select the **ONE** response that corrects this error.

(8) Birds [A) was singing / B) sings / C) had sang / D) sing] to attract mates or mark their territory.

A) was singing
B) sings
C) had sang
D) sing

Julia has made an error in sentence 10. Select the **ONE** response that corrects this error.

(10) When you watch TV or play video games, sound energy makes the experience [A) better. / B) more good. / C) goodest. / D) most better.]

A) better.
B) more good.
C) goodest.
D) most better.

#5 What is the correct way to write sentence 15?

(15) These loud sounds use sound energy to warn people this helps keep them safe.

A) These loud sounds use sound energy to warn people, and this helps. Keep them safe.
B) These loud sounds use sound energy to warn people, this helps keep them safe.
C) These loud sounds use sound energy to warn people and help keep them safe.
D) These loud sounds use sound energy. To warn people. This helps keep them safe.

EDITING: PRACTICE #5B

Maya is writing a story for her science class. Read these paragraphs from the body of Maya's paper and look for corrections she needs to make. Then answer the questions that follow.

Gravity's Pull

(1) Dana decided to do some experiments. She found a feather and a rock. (2) First, she dropped the feather. (3) It floated gently down to the ground. (4) Next, she dropped the rock. (5) It fell quickly it landed with a thud. (6) Dana was fascinated. (7) "Why did the rock fall faster than the feather?" she asked.

(8) Her dad explained, "Both the feather and the rock are pulled by gravity. (9) The feather falls slow because of air resistance. (10) The air is pushing up against the feather. (11) The rock is more heavy and doesn't get slowed down as much by the air."

(12) Excited by her new knowledge, Dana climbed up a small tree and carefully dropped different objects. (13) She dropped a small toy car a leaf, and an apple. (14) She noticed that the toy car and the apple fell straight down quickly. (15) The leaf fluttered slowly, just like the feather. (16) She saw that gravity pulled everything down. (17) Lighter objects with more air resistance fell more slowly.

(18) Danas final experiment was with a piece of paper. (19) She crumpled one piece into a ball and left another flat. (20) She dropped them at the same time. (21) The crumpled paper ball fell quickly, while the flat piece of paper drifted down slowly. (22) Dana laughed. (23) She realized that air resistance makes a big difference in how things fall.

#1 What is the correct way to write sentence 5?

(5) It fell quickly it landed with a thud.

A) It fell quickly and landed with a thud.
B) It fell quickly. And landed with a thud.
C) It fell quickly, it landed with a thud.
D) It fell quickly. It landed. With a thud.

What change should be made in sentence 9?

(9) The feather falls slow because of air resistance.

A) Change **falls** to **falled**
B) Change **slow** to **slowly**
C) Change **because** to **be cause**
D) Change the period to a question mark

Maya has made an error in sentence 11. Select the **ONE** response that corrects this error.

(11) The rock is
A) heaviest
B) less heavy
C) heavier
D) most heavy
and doesn't get slowed down as much by the air."

What change should be made in sentence 13?

(13) She dropped a small toy car a leaf, and an apple.

A) Change **dropped** to **droped**
B) Change **small** to **smallest**
C) Insert a comma after **car**
D) Change **apple** to **appel**

What change should be made in sentence 18?

(18) Danas final experiment was with a piece of paper.

A) Change **Danas** to **Dana's**
B) Change **was** to **were**
C) Change **with** to **for**
D) Change **piece** to **peace**

EDITING: WARM-UP #6

Amir is writing a paper for his social studies class. Read these paragraphs from the beginning of Amir's paper and look for corrections he needs to make. Then answer the questions that follow.

Carmen's Civic Responsibility

(1) Carmen felt sad seeing her favorite park so messy. (2) She remembered her teacher talking about civic responsibility. (3) This means doing things to help your community. (4) Carmen decided she could make a difference, even if she was just one person. (5) She ran home, grabbed some supplys, and set off to the park.

(6) At the park, Carmen began picking up the trash. (7) She careful collected each piece and put it in her garbage bag. (8) It was hard work, but she knew it was important to keep the park clean and safe for everyone. (9) As she worked, some of her friends saw what she was doing and came over to help. (10) Soon, the park looked more better.

(11) When they finished, Carmen felt proud of what they had done. (12) The park was clean again. (13) She new that everyone would enjoy playing there without the trash. (14) Carmen's friends thanked her for starting the clean-up, and they all agreed to remind each other to pick up after themselves in the future.

(15) Later that week, Carmen's teacher asked if anyone had done something special for their community. (16) Carmen shared her story, and her classmates claped for her. (17) They were inspired by her act of civic responsibility and wanted to help their community too.

What change should be made in sentence 5?

(5) She ran home, grabbed some supplys, and set off to the park.

A) Delete the comma after **home**
B) Change **grabbed** to **grabs**
C) Change **supplys** to **supplies**
D) Change **and** to **or**

What change should be made in sentence 7?

(7) She careful collected each piece and put it in her garbage bag.

A) Change **careful** to **carefully**
B) Change **collected** to **collecting**
C) Change **in** to **over**
D) Change **her** to **she's**

Amir has made an error in sentence 10. Select the **ONE** response that corrects this error.

(10) Soon, the park looked

A) most better.
B) better.
C) more good.
D) best.

What change should be made in sentence 13?

(13) She new that everyone would enjoy playing there without the trash.

A) Change **new** to **knew**
B) Change **everyone** to **every one**
C) Change **would** to **wouldn't**
D) Change **enjoy** to **injoy**

What change should be made in sentence 16?

(16) Carmen shared her story, and her classmates claped for her.

A) Change **shared** to **shares**
B) Remove the comma after **story**
C) Change **classmates** to **Classmates**
D) Change **claped** to **clapped**

EDITING: PRACTICE #6A

Sabrina is writing a paper for her social studies class. Read these paragraphs from the body of Sabrina's paper and look for corrections she needs to make. Then answer the questions that follow.

Safety in a Community

(1) When people live together, they can protect each other from dangers like wild animals, bad weather, or other things that might want to cause harm. (2) They can built strong shelters and work together to stay safe.

(3) In communities, people can share important things like food water, and tools. (4) When people work together, they can make sure that everyone has what they need to live well.

(5) Living in a community means that people can help each other when needed. (6) If someone is sick or needs help building a house, others in the community who can lend a hand. (7) This makes life more easy and more safe for everyone.

(8) Communities make rules to keep everyone safe and to make sure things run smooth. (9) These rules help prevent fights and protect people's rights so everyone can live together peacefully.

(10) Sometimes, communities have to protect them selves from attacks by others. (11) By living together, people can form a group to defend their homes and keep their community safe.

What change should be made in sentence 2?

(2) They can built strong shelters and work together to stay safe.

A) Change **built** to **build**
B) Change **strong** to **strongest**
C) Change **shelters** to **shelter's**
D) Insert a comma after **water**

What change should be made in sentence 3?

(3) In communities, people can share important things like food water, and tools.

A) Change **can** to **can't**
B) Change **things** to **thing**
C) Insert a comma after **food**
D) Delete the comma after **water**

#3 Sabrina has made an error in sentence 7. Select the **ONE** response that corrects this error.

(7) This makes life [A) easier and safer / B) more easy and more safe / C) easily and safely / D) most easy and most safe] for everyone.

A) easier and safer
B) more easy and more safe
C) easily and safely
D) most easy and most safe

#4 What change should be made in sentence 8?

(8) Communities make rules to keep everyone safe and to make sure things run smooth.

A) Change **make** to **makes**
B) Change **everyone** to **every one**
C) Insert a comma after **safe**
D) Change **smooth** to **smoothly**

#5 What change should be made in sentence 10?

(10) Sometimes, communities have to protect them selves from attacks by others.

A) Change **communities** to **communitys**
B) Change **have** to **has**
C) Change **them selves** to **themselves**
D) Change **others** to **other's**

EDITING: PRACTICE #6B

Sherry is writing a paper for her social studies class. Read these paragraphs from the body of Sherry's paper and look for corrections she needs to make. Then answer the questions that follow.

Recreation

(1) One of the most popular places for recreation is the local park. (2) Parks are greatest because they have open spaces. (3) People can play sports like soccer baseball, or frisbee. (4) Many parks also have playgrounds with swings, slides, and climbing structures. (5) Some parks even have picnic areas where families can gather and enjoy nature.

(6) Another way people meet their recreational needs is by going to community centers. (7) These centers often have gyms, swimming pools, and places to take classes. (8) People of all ages can join these activitys to learn new skills and spend time with others.

(9) Libraries are also important for recreation. (10) They're known for books, but many libraries offer programs like storytime, crafts, and movie nights. (11) These activities provide a fun and educational way for people to spend their free time and explore new hobby.

(12) Sports are another way people in the community have fun. (13) Kids and adults can join teams to play basketball, soccer, or baseball. (14) These leagues give people the chance to be part of a team and compete in games. (15) It's a great way to stay actively and meet new friends.

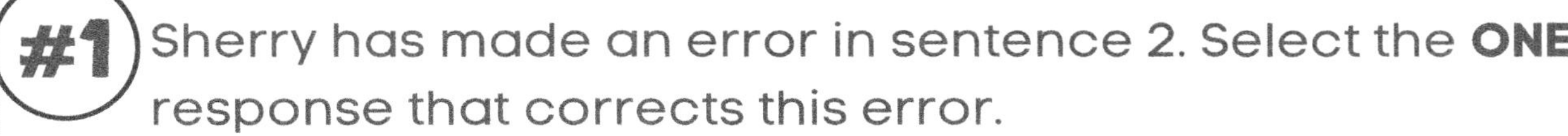

#1 Sherry has made an error in sentence 2. Select the **ONE** response that corrects this error.

(2) Parks are [A) great / B) more greater / C) most great / D) greatly] because they have open spaces.

- A) great
- B) more greater
- C) most great
- D) greatly

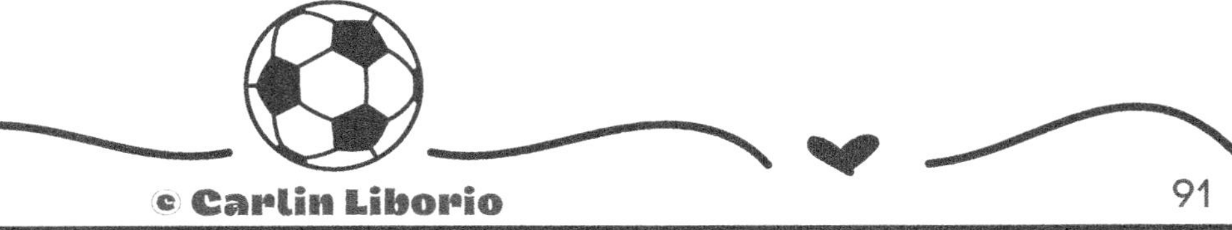

What change should be made in sentence 3?

(3) People can play sports like soccer baseball, or frisbee.

A) Change **People** to **Persons**
B) Change **soccer** to **Soccer**
C) Insert a comma after **soccer**
D) Change the **period** to a **question mark**

What change should be made in sentence 8?

(8) People of all ages can join these activitys to learn new skills and spend time with others.

A) Change **can** to **can't**
B) Change **these** to **this**
C) Change **activitys** to **activities**
D) Change **others** to **other's**

What change should be made in sentence 11?

(11) These activities provide a fun and educational way for people to spend their free time and explore new hobby.

A) Change **activities** to **activitys**
B) Change **spend** to **spent**
C) Change **their** to **they're**
D) Change **hobby** to **hobbies**

What change should be made in sentence 15?

(15) It's a great way to stay actively and meet new friends.

A) Change **way** to **ways**
B) Change **actively** to **active**
C) Change **new** to **knew**
D) Change **friends** to **friend's**

EDITING: WARM-UP #7

Janelle is writing a paper for her science class. Read these paragraphs from the body of Janelle's paper and look for corrections she needs to make. Then answer the questions that follow.

The Food Chain

(1) At the start of the food chain are plants. (2) Plants are speshul because they can make their own food using the sun's energy. (3) This process is called photosynthesis. (4) Plants take in sunlight, water, and carbon dioxide from the air to make their food. (5) Energy stored inside them. (6) Because they make their own food, plants are called producers.

(7) Next in the food chain are animals that eat plants. (8) These animals are called herbivores they are the first consumers in the food chain. (9) For example, imagine a rabbit nibbling on some grass. (10) The rabbit eats the grass to get the energy that the plant made using the sun. (11) The energy that was stored in the plant now flows into the rabbit.

(12) The food chain doesn't stop there! (13) Some animals eat other animals to get energy. (14) These animals are called carnivores. (15) For instance, a fox might catch and eat the rabbit. (16) When the fox eats the rabbit, the energy that was in the rabbit now flows past the fox. (17) This energy helps the fox run, hunt, and stay healthy. (18) The fox is a second consumer in the food chain.

(19) At the end of the food chain are decomposers, like fungi and bacteria. (20) When plants and animals die, decomposers break down there bodies and return nutrients to the soil. (21) This helps plants grow, starting the food chain all over again.

Sentence 2 is written incorrectly. Select the **ONE** response that corrects this sentence.

(2) Plants are

A) speshal
B) spaciel
C) spashel
D) special

because they can make their own food using the sun's energy.

#2 Sentence 5 is written incorrectly. Select the **ONE** response that corrects this sentence.

(5) [A) This is the / B) The / C) Using the / D) This is it. The] energy stored inside them.

A) This is the
B) The
C) Using the
D) This is it. The

#3 Which is the correct way to write sentence 8?

(8) These animals are called herbivores they are the first consumers in the food chain.

A) These animals are called herbivores, they are the first consumers in the food chain.
B) These animals are called herbivores, yet they are the first consumers in the food chain.
C) These animals are called herbivores, and they are the first consumers in the. food chain.
D) These animals are called herbivores, but they are the first consumers in the food chain.

#4 Janelle has written sentence 16 incorrectly. Select the **ONE** response that corrects this sentence.

(16) When the fox eats the rabbit, the energy that was in the rabbit now flows [A) above / B) into / C) under / D) beside] the fox.

A) above
B) into
C) under
D) beside

#5 What change should be made in sentence 20?

(20) When plants and animals die, decomposers break down there bodies and return nutrients to the soil.

A) Change **animals** to **animal's**
B) Change **there** to **their**
C) Change **bodies** to **bodys**
D) Insert a comma after **bodies**

EDITING: PRACTICE #7A

Kathleen is writing a paper for her science class. Read these paragraphs from the body of Kathleen's paper and look for corrections she needs to make. Then answer the questions that follow.

Droughts and the Environment

(1) Imagine a long hot summer with hardly any rain. (2) The grass turns brown, the streams dry up, and the ground becomes hard and cracked. (3) This is what happens until a drought. (4) A drought is a period with much less rain than usual. (5) Droughts can be tough on plants and animals. (6) Did you know that some organisms actually thrive during droughts. (7) Let's explore how this happens.

(8) First, let's talk about plants. (9) In normal conditions, many plants need a lot of water too grow. (10) But during a drought, the lack of water can cause these plants to wilt and die. (11) However, some special plants are builded to survive with very little water. (12) Cacti are a great example. (13) Cacti have thick, fleshy stems that store water. (14) They have tiny or no leaves to reduce water loss. (15) In a drought, cacti and similar plants can continue to grow while other plants struggle.

(16) Other organisms might struggle but drought-tolerant plants have an advantage. (17) With less competition for resources like water and food, they can thrive. (18) For instance, as other plants die off, cacti might have more space to grow and more sunlight to absorb. (19) Similarly, animals like kangaroo rats might find it easier to gather food because other animals are struggling to survive.

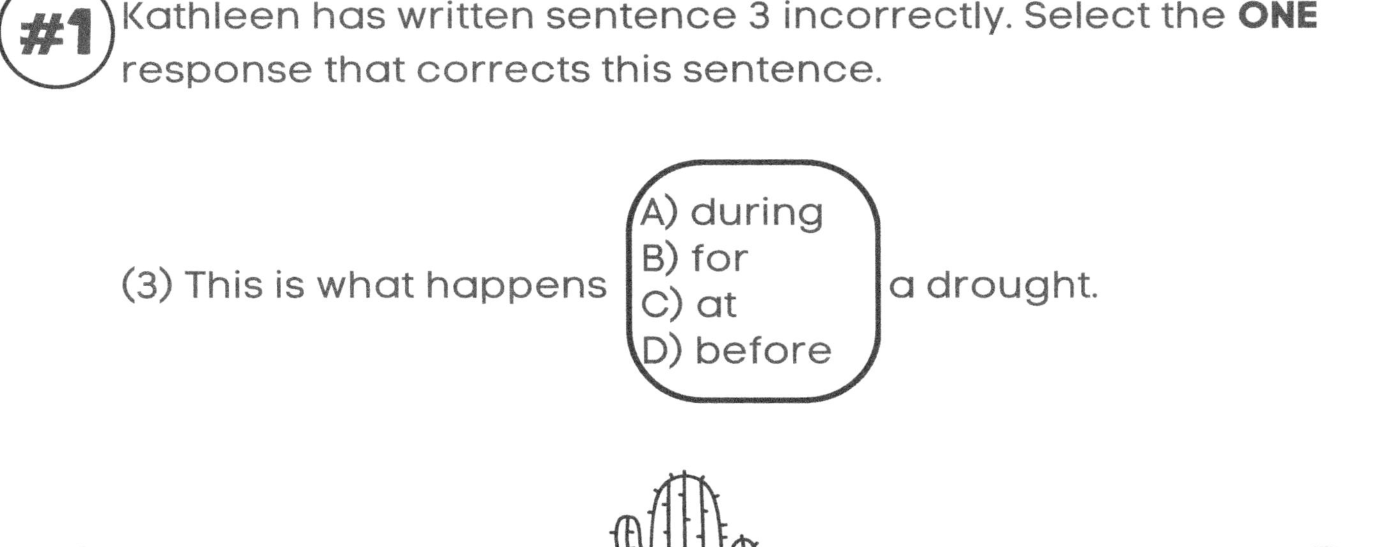

#1 Kathleen has written sentence 3 incorrectly. Select the **ONE** response that corrects this sentence.

(3) This is what happens [A) during / B) for / C) at / D) before] a drought.

A) during
B) for
C) at
D) before

#2 What change should be made in sentence 6?

(6) Did you know that some organisms actually thrive during droughts.

A) Change **know** to **no**
B) Change **organisms** to **organism**
C) Change **thrive** to **thriving**
D) Change the **period** to a **question mark**

#3 What change should be made in sentence 9?

(9) In normal conditions, many plants need a lot of water too grow.

A) Change **In** to **After**
B) Change **conditions** to **condishuns**
C) Change **too** to **to**
D) Change the **period** to a **question mark**

#4 What change should be made in sentence 11?

(11) However, some special plants are builded to survive with very little water.

A) Change **special** to **speshul**
B) Change **plants** to **plant's**
C) Change **are** to **will be**
D) Change **builded** to **built**

#5 Which is the correct way to write sentence 16?

(16) Other organisms might struggle but drought-tolerant plants have an advantage.

A) Other organisms might struggle, drought-tolerant plants have an advantage.
B) Other organisms might struggle, but drought-tolerant plants have an advantage.
C) Other organisms might struggle before drought-tolerant plants have an advantage.
D) Other organisms might struggle because drought-tolerant plants have an advantage.

EDITING: PRACTICE #7B

Tammy is writing a paper for her science class. Read these paragraphs from the beginning of Tammy's paper and look for corrections she needs to make. Then answer the questions that follow.

Koko the Chimp

(1) Let's take a journey to the rainforest, where we can find one of the smartest animals on Earth—the chimpanzee. (2) Chimpanzees are amazing creatures. (3) One of the reasons they is so special is because they know how to use tools.

(4) One day, a young chimpanzee named Koko feeled hungry. (5) He knew there was something tasty hidden inside a tall termite mound nearby. (6) Termites are small insects that build huge mounds out of dirt, and chimpanzees love to eat them. (7) But there was a problem. (8) The termites were deep inside the mound. (9) Couldn't reach them with his fingers.

(10) Koko thought for a moment and then had a clever idea. (11) He looked around and found a long thin stick on the ground. (12) He picked up the stick and starts to poke it carefully into the small holes in the termite mound. (13) At first, nothing happened, but Koko was patient. (14) He wiggled the stick around inside the hole, and soon, the termites started to crawl onto the stick.

(15) When Koko pulled the stick out of the mound, it was covered in termites! (16) He quickly licked them off the stick and enjoyed his snack. (17) Koko had used the stick as a tool to help him get food that he couldnt reach on his own. (18) This is an example of an animal using a tool!

#1 Tammy has written sentence 3 incorrectly. Select the **ONE** response that corrects this sentence.

(3) One of the reasons [A) they's / B) they'd / C) they've / D) they're] so special is because they know how to use tools.

A) they's
B) they'd
C) they've
D) they're

What change should be made in sentence 4?

(4) One day, a young chimpanzee named Koko feeled hungry.

A) Change **named** to **names**
B) Change **Koko** to **koko**
C) Change **feeled** to **felt**
D) Change the **period** to a **question mark**

#3 Tammy has written sentence 9 incorrectly. Select the **ONE** response that corrects this sentence.

(9) [A) And / B) Koko / C) The termites / D) Deep inside, and] couldn't reach them with his fingers.

#4 What change should be made in sentence 12?

(12) He picked up the stick and starts to poke it carefully into the small holes in the termite mound.

A) Change **starts** to **started**
B) Change **carefully** to **careful**
C) Change **small** to **more small**
D) Change the **period** to a **question mark**

#5 What change should be made in sentence 17?

(17) Koko had used the stick as a tool to help him get food that he couldnt reach on his own.

A) Change **used** to **use**
B) Change **tool** to **tools**
C) Change **help** to **helps**
D) Change **couldnt** to **couldn't**

Revise	Edit
ARMS	CUPS
A Add sentences and words.	**C** Capitals: sentences, names, places, months, titles, I
R Remove words or sentences.	**U** Usage: match nouns and verbs correctly, grammar usage
M Move a word or sentence.	**P** Punctuation: . ! ? ' , " "
S Substitute words or sentences.	**S** Spelling: Check all words, use your resources.

© Carlin Liborio

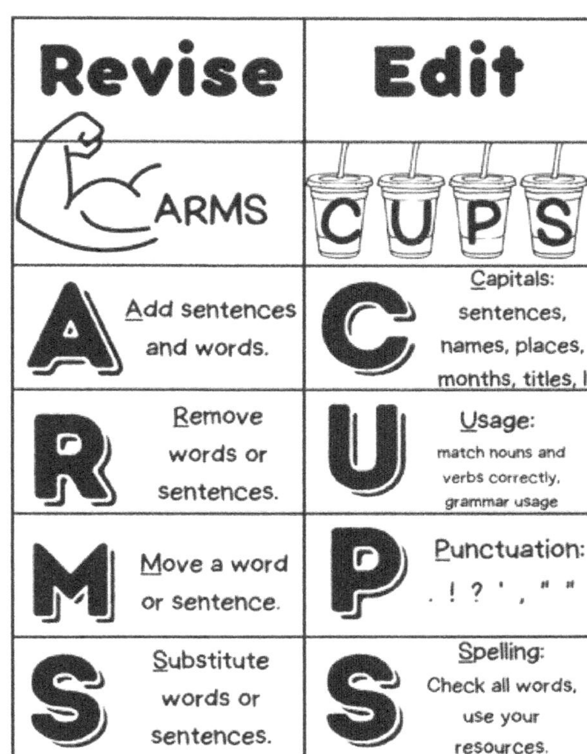
Revise	Edit
ARMS	CUPS
A Add sentences and words.	**C** Capitals: sentences, names, places, months, titles, I
R Remove words or sentences.	**U** Usage: match nouns and verbs correctly, grammar usage
M Move a word or sentence.	**P** Punctuation: . ! ? ' , " "
S Substitute words or sentences.	**S** Spelling: Check all words, use your resources.

© Carlin Liborio

Revise	Edit
ARMS	CUPS
A Add sentences and words.	**C** Capitals: sentences, names, places, months, titles, I
R Remove words or sentences.	**U** Usage: match nouns and verbs correctly, grammar usage
M Move a word or sentence.	**P** Punctuation: . ! ? ' , " "
S Substitute words or sentences.	**S** Spelling: Check all words, use your resources.

© Carlin Liborio

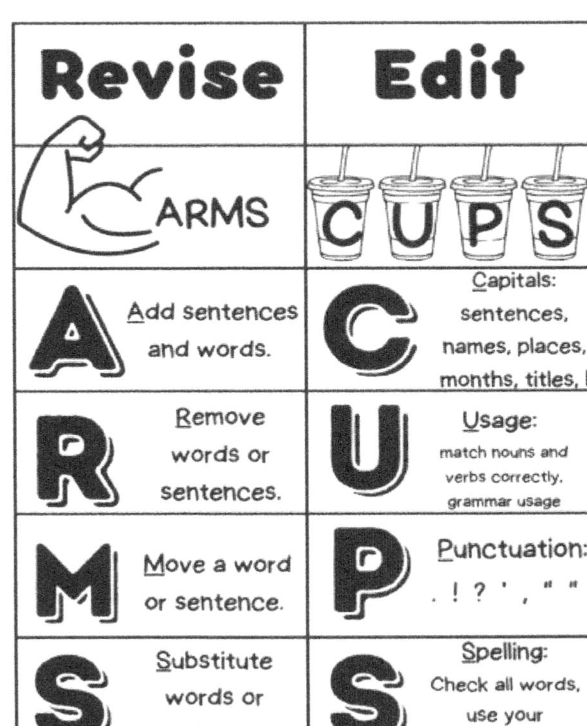
Revise	Edit
ARMS	CUPS
A Add sentences and words.	**C** Capitals: sentences, names, places, months, titles, I
R Remove words or sentences.	**U** Usage: match nouns and verbs correctly, grammar usage
M Move a word or sentence.	**P** Punctuation: . ! ? ' , " "
S Substitute words or sentences.	**S** Spelling: Check all words, use your resources.

© Carlin Liborio

3RD GRADE REVISING ANSWER KEYS

WARM-UP #1

1.	B
2.	**Sample Answer:** Some folks might be sick or hungry.
3.	C
4.	D
5.	A

WARM-UP #2

1.	**Sample Answer:** You can have some money for spending, saving, and donating.
2.	D
3.	C
4.	A
5.	B

WARM-UP #3

1.	**Sample Answer:** He guided his local community and nation in many ways.
2.	**Sample Answer:** During the American Revolution, Franklin showed great leadership.
3.	A
4.	D
5.	B

WARM-UP #4

1.	B
2.	**Sample Answer:** During this time, families create beautiful altars with colorful flowers, shiny candles, and delicious food.
3.	B
4.	C
5.	**Sample Answer:** The Day of the Dead is a special time for families to be close, eat yummy food, and share stories.

WARM-UP #5

1.	B
2.	C
3.	D
4.	D
5.	**Sample Answer**: They even planted flowers and added benches to make it even more beautiful.

WARM-UP #6

1.	B
2.	A
3.	**Sample Answer:** It's a mystery how the stones got there and why they were placed that way.
4.	D
5.	D

WARM-UP #7

1.	B
2.	D
3.	B
4.	A
5.	D

PRACTICE #1

1.	B	6.	A
2.	D	7.	D
3.	D	8.	B
4.	A	9.	C
5.	B	10.	**Sample Answer**: We learned that even though we are just kids, we can make a big difference by helping those in need.

PRACTICE #2

1.	C	6.	A
2.	A	7.	D
3.	**Sample Answer:** Donating helps others, like giving to a charity.	8.	B
4.	B	9.	**Sample Answer:** Plus, I learned that even as a kid, I can make a positive impact on the world by giving back.
5.	B	10.	A

3RD GRADE REVISING ANSWER KEYS

PRACTICE #3

1.	B	6.	C
2.	**Sample Answer:** But Daniel Boone was different. **OR** However, Daniel Boone was different.	7.	D
3.	C	8.	**Sample Answer:** To protect themselves, they built a fort. **OR** They build a fort to protect themselves.
4.	A	9.	A
5.	B	10.	C

PRACTICE #4

1.	C	6.	C
2.	D	7.	A
3.	A	8.	B
4.	B	9.	D
5.	**Sample Answer:** At the temple, monks led the group in special prayers.	10.	**Sample Answer:** It reminded her of the importance of family, tradition, and kindness.

PRACTICE #5

1.	A	6.	B
2.	B	7.	C
3.	A	8.	**Sample Answers:** A group of students and teachers decides to clean up a polluted river. **OR** A group of students and teachers has decided to clean a polluted river.
4.	**Sample Answer:** Over time, more folks join in, and soon the whole town is covered in greenery.	9.	B
5.	D	10.	D

PRACTICE #6

1.	A	6.	B
2.	D	7.	C
3.	B	8.	B
4.	**Sample Answer:** In 2005, Hurricane Katrina crossed the southern tip of Florida and moved into the Gulf. **OR** Hurricane Katrina crossed the southern tip of Florida and moved into the Gulf in 2005.	9.	A
5.	D	10.	**Sample Answer:** After the storm has passed, they return home to all the benefits that come with living on the Gulf Coast.

PRACTICE #7

1.	C	6.	B
2.	D	7.	**Sample Answer**: They loved getting such comfy boots at a lower price.
3.	A	8.	A
4.	D	9.	C
5.	B	10.	B

3RD GRADE EDITING ANSWER KEYS

WARM-UP #1

1.	A
2.	C
3.	C
4.	A
5.	B

PRACTICE #1A

1.	C
2.	A
3.	C
4.	B
5.	B

PRACTICE #1B

1.	D
2.	D
3.	A
4.	C
5.	C

WARM-UP #2

1.	D
2.	C
3.	A
4.	B
5.	A

PRACTICE #2A

1.	C
2.	D
3.	B
4.	A
5.	C

PRACTICE #2B

1.	B
2.	D
3.	A
4.	C
5.	B

WARM-UP #3

1.	A
2.	C
3.	D
4.	A
5.	D

PRACTICE #3A

1.	D
2.	A
3.	A
4.	B
5.	C

PRACTICE #3B

1.	A
2.	C
3.	D
4.	C
5.	B

WARM-UP #4

1.	D
2.	B
3.	D
4.	D
5.	C

PRACTICE #4A

1.	D
2.	A
3.	B
4.	C
5.	D

PRACTICE #4B

1.	A
2.	C
3.	C
4.	D
5.	D

3RD GRADE EDITING ANSWER KEYS

WARM-UP #5

1.	C
2.	B
3.	C
4.	A
5.	B

PRACTICE #5A

1.	B
2.	D
3.	D
4.	A
5.	C

PRACTICE #5B

1.	A
2.	B
3.	C
4.	C
5.	A

WARM-UP #6

1.	C
2.	A
3.	B
4.	A
5.	D

PRACTICE #6A

1.	A
2.	C
3.	A
4.	D
5.	C

PRACTICE #6B

1.	A
2.	C
3.	C
4.	D
5.	B

WARM-UP #7

1.	D
2.	A
3.	C
4.	B
5.	B

PRACTICE #7A

1.	A
2.	D
3.	C
4.	D
5.	B

PRACTICE #7B

1.	D
2.	C
3.	B
4.	A
5.	D

Made in the USA
Coppell, TX
11 February 2026